Memories of a Small-Town Yankee

Memories of a

Small-Town Yankee

By Kenneth G. Richards

Millers River Publishing Co.
Athol, Massachusetts

Library of Congress Catalog Card Number 84-062286
International Standard Book Number (ISBN) 0-912395-04-4

Published by Millers River Publishing Co.
P.O. Box 159
Athol, Massachusetts

Manufactured in the United States of America
First edition. First printing, January 1985.

Cover photograph courtesy Dick Chaisson Collection
Cover design by Patience Bundschuh

FOR MY CHILDREN

Glenn, Stacy, Elizabeth and Mitchell

and

for theirs

and

for theirs

Table of Contents

Preface

This book did not start out to be a book at all. It began at the suggestion of my oldest son as simply the act of putting down on paper some of the family stories that I have been repeating to my children for a generation. Some are tales that have been passed down from my father and a few, perhaps, even from his father. But most are of my experiences while growing up in New England in the '30s and '40s and a few are "sea stories" of my first hitch in the Navy during World War II.

Much of the material in this book appeared in a series of short articles in the Athol Daily News in the spring of 1984. It was that series that prompted publisher Allen Young to suggest a book.

As I prepared the book manuscript, there was a natural writer's urge to smooth out the transitions from subject to subject — to structure the book in some sort of traditional form. Yet, I wanted to retain the impression of one side of a dialogue between old friends reminiscing about old times. It came to me, finally, that conversations about the good old days simply are not structured. They skip across time and dart abruptly from subject to subject without any obvious logic. Such conversations go something like this:

"Do you remember old ——— who used to sit next to me in Miss Ryan's class? He lives over in Orange now. His youngest son is married to ———. Her mother is ———. Use to live up on Brattle Street. You remember her. She was in our class at Riverbend School ——— the one with the big ———. Her older brother ——— was killed at Salerno. He used to run around with old ———. Drove a 1932 Studebaker coupe. I remember the time we took that old Studebaker out to Cape Cod ———" And so on.

To pause and structure our recollections would be next to impossible and in any case would spoil the fun. So I have resisted the urge for structured progression and form. While I have tried to keep my stories in some sort of chronological order, I have forsaken many of the traditional rules that authors are expected to follow. In so doing, I hope that I have preserved some of the flavor and spontaneity of a conversation between old friends.

There was a temptation, also, to try to verify dates and names and places and other facts. But that I resisted also. The events, the people, and the places portrayed in this book are drawn entirely from my memory. Others may remember the particulars of those same events, people, and places much differently. That's a nice thing about personal memories – the passing years tend to shape and mold the facts to fit comfortably within the framework of our individual experiences.

The most important thing, I think, is to enjoy our memories and especially the sharing of them. I hope my enjoyment at the opportunity to share my memories comes through in the telling.

Kenneth G. Richards
Pebble Beach, California
September 1984

Chapter 1

'Who D'Ya Think Y'Ar' – Tom Mix?'

When I received a copy of Allen Young's delightful and informative book "North of Quabbin," I found myself recalling long forgotten scenes and events of my childhood. It's been more than 36 years since I lived in that lovely area north of Quabbin and I have been back only three or four times for very brief visits.

Browsing through Young's book is a real nostalgia trip for an old expatriate. The names and photographs stir bright memories of my childhood years. They are memories of a life and time that seem, in retrospect, to have been idyllic and carefree. Such images are somewhat gilded, of course, but memory has a wonderful capacity for gradually smoothing out the rough edges of reality and providing a softer, rosier hue to childhood scenes. And, too, memory has a way of exaggerating things. The summers become hotter, the winters colder, the fish bigger, the cars faster, the escapades more death-defying, the work harder, the good times more fun, the hard times more difficult, the moral codes more strict, the discipline more severe. Be that as it may, an occasional "walk down memory lane" in middle age renews the spirit and satisfies the need to reaffirm one's roots.

I'm proud of my Yankee heritage and I recall my childhood in the Athol area with great affection. I like to think, though, that my New England accent has softened through the years. Still, a question I am frequently asked by new acquaintances is, "Are you from Boston?" Apparently you can take the boy out of New England but you can't take the New England out of the boy.

"No, I'm not from Boston," I reply. (Why do people think that just because you say "Hahvud" or "connuh" or "cah" that you have to be from Boston?) "I'm from up around Athol," I tell them.

"Oh yeah," some say, "I've heard the joke." They then proceed to repeat that absurd story about the lisping train conductor. Will that puny pun ever die a natural death?

Old Clippings

After reading Young's book I dug out my old footlocker that is crammed with souvenirs and mementos of my early life — snapshots, newspaper clippings, memorabilia of places I visited and events I attended, old maps, certificates, trophies, and innumerable other objects that only I can appreciate.

Most of the newspaper clippings that I have are, of course, from the Athol Daily News. All my clippings concern my family or friends —

marriages, deaths, graduations, etc. I suppose it is the personal stories and items that make the small-town newspaper so valuable and cherished in a community. I remember as a child that there were few things in our daily lives quite so satisfying as having someone say, "I saw your name in the Daily News yesterday."

While the Athol Daily News never had a society page or column that I recall, it did frequently run little items about Atholians who traveled. It didn't have to be very far. A typical item might read "Mr. and Mrs. So-and-So with daughter Susie caught the 7:28 train to Boston yesterday where they shopped and did some sightseeing. They returned on the 9:35 last evening."

This, I considered to be the epitome of social recognition and I longed for the day when I could get my name in the paper like that. Finally, around 1939 or so, my grandfather took my brother and me by train to Boston to see the circus. I think I imagined that an Athol Daily News reporter would be at the station to interview us. No such luck, of course, and to my disappointment I never did "make" the Daily News for being a world traveler. I did, however get my name in the paper on a few occasions. Each time an Athol student made five book reports at school his achievement was published in the Daily News. My family and relatives always made a great to-do about that and I basked in their praise. Still, this somehow didn't carry the social significance of a travel item.

'Boy Allies' and Other Books

I was an avid reader in my childhood. I remember the attic of the Carey house, which we rented for a year or so on Wilder Street, was filled with children's books. There were many in the "Boy Allies" series (about two young Americans who fought in every phase and battle of the First World War). There were a lot of the Tom Swift books about his submarine and electric runabout, etc. And of course there were the ever delighful Edward Lear nonsense books about the Owl and the Pussycat, and the Quangle Wangle's Hat, and the Courtship of the Yonghy-Bongy-Bo, and the Dong with the Luminous Nose. We read of the "great Gromboolian plain" and the "hills of the Chankly Bore" and our imaginations were tested to their limits in trying to imagine what a "Pobble" or a "Jumblie" or a "Yonghy-Bongy-Bo" looked like.

And then of course there were the Thornton Burgess nature books.

His wonderful stories have stayed with me ever since. And I've discovered, I'm not the only one of my generation as impressed with the Burgess books. I recall the following incident that really highlights, for me, Burgess' lasting influence on American kids:

Occasionally, I find myself part of a group of middle-aged "arm chair generals" who sit around discussing such topics as the tactical shortcomings of Georgie Patton and Montgomery and Bull Halsey in "Dubya Dubya Two." It's a shame that Ike or MacArthur or Nimitz never thought to call on us for advice at the time. Had they sought our widsom there might never have been a Battle of the Bulge or Monte Cassino or Iwo Jima. And we very likely could have turned Pearl Harbor into a resounding victory.

Anyway, a couple of years ago we were trying to impress each other with our military genius when there came about as quick a change of subject as you'll ever see. Someone mentioned that if Rommel was the "Desert Fox" then Montgomery was "Chatterer the Red Squirrel." Someone immediately recognized the name as a character from Thornton Burgess' wonderful series of nature stories and said, "Yeah, or Sammy Jay!" As every fan of Thornton Burgess knows, both Chatterer and Sammy were noisy, obnoxious animal characters. Someone else added a name and soon it became a challenge to see how many of the Burgess charaters we could remember. All thoughts of military leaders were quickly out of mind. We all had been children in the '30s and each had been an avid Thornton Burgess reader. We moved to a room with a chalkboard and began listing the names — Peter Rabbit, Jimmy Skunk, Mother West Wind, the Green Forest, the Green Meadows, Farmer Brown, Farmer Brown's Son (I think Burgess never did reveal the boy's name), Laughing Brook, Smiling Pool, Hooty the Owl, Danny Meadowmouse, and many more. I've forgotten the number we finally ended up with but the list stayed on the chalkboard for weeks and passersby would sometimes add a name. I think a few contributions were ringers — names that no one could confirm or deny, but it was nice to find so many people (young, old and middle-aged) who share such a pleasant common bond.

Now if only the real generals of the great powers could be as easily distracted from military matters and turn instead to the themes of Thornton Burgess, our world might be a nicer, safer place to live!

In my box of souvenirs I found a little photographic album, dated 1935, of my third grade class at Main Street School in Athol. Can that

"Those bright and smiling faces." Third grade at Main Street School, Athol, 1935. From left to right, top row — August Bagdonas, Cecil Bosworth, Alice Duguay; second row — Norman Dill, Cynthia Kimball, William Killay; third row — Charles Plotkin, Alice Rayner, Ernest Ricard; bottom — the author, Mary Robesauskas, Robert Truehart.

skinny kid with his hair parted in the middle really be me? I scan those bright and smiling faces and wonder what they look like and where they are now. I remember many of their names — there's Jack Rist, Billy Killay, Cynthia Kimball, August Bagdonas, Charlie Plotkin, Cecil Bosworth, and Shirley Thompson to name a few. And there's that boy named Albin who once caused a big stir in town because it was feared that he had been kidnapped. He disappeared and people reported a mysterious black car in the vicinity where he was last seen. The Lindberg kidnapping was still very much on people's minds and ominous rumors were rampant in the area. He was found safe and sound a couple days later, however, with relatives who had not seen the glaring headlines in the Athol Daily News.

Another picture in my 1935 school album is of the pretty bright-eyed little girl who was the first girl ever to express a fondness for me. To say that we were sweethearts would be a gross exaggeration. However, in a moment of adolescent passion I once punched her in the stomach as a heartfelt, if indelicate, expression of my undying love. She reminded me of that incident many years later. By then, however, she was engaged to a young man who presumably did not resort to physical violence in his courtship.

On The Radio

Remembering that year of 1935 reminds me of the kids' radio shows that were so popular. While it is difficult for our younger generation today to imagine a world without television, children of my generation were hooked on radio. I remember such programs as Amos 'n' Andy, Jack Armstrong ("The Alllllll-American Boy"), and Little Orphan Annie. But I think that the most popular of all was the Tom Mix program that came on about suppertime each weeknight. I'm sure most of us today can still sing a few bars of the theme song (set to the tune of "Roundup Time in Texas" — substitute "Ralston" for "roundup" and "breakfast" for "Texas"). We all solemnly took the Tom Mix Ralston Straight Shooter pledge, promising, as I recall, to "shoot straight" with Mom and Dad by being a good kid and with our friends by always playing fair and square (and being a good loser if necessary). We also pledged to shoot straight with Tom Mix by eating good ol' Ralston every morning which, of course, was the whole point of the program.

When we played "cowboys" everyone wanted to "be" Tom Mix

who was automatically assumed to be the leader of any posse. No one wanted to be the other characters from the Tom Mix radio show like the Old Wrangler or Tom's kid friends Jimmy and Jane with whom we were supposed to identify. Fortunately, there were other cowboy heroes to "be" and I usually chose to be Ken Maynard, the "Arizona Kid" since we shared the same first name. My brother Norm was Buck Jones, my brother Mac was Hoot Gibson, and my sister Mary was Gene Autrey. Some kids played being Charles Starrett, the "Durango Kid" (Athol's own movie star), or Hopalong Cassidy, or the Long Ranger.

In our estimation, however, Tom Mix stood a head taller than all the other heroes of the day. He could do anything, we thought. They finally had to bring in a guy from another planet to out-do him. But, until Superman came along, the standard put-down for any kid who boasted too much was, "Who d'ya think you are – Tom Mix?"

We didn't have many fancy cowboy get-ups but a colorful bandana was a must. We wore it across our nose and tied behind our neck even if we were playing good guys (which we almost always were – in those days the bad guys invariably lost). Some of us had toy rifles but most of us had pistols and, like the movie cowboys of that era, we could fire our six-shooters 20 or 30 times without reloading. They just don't make guns like that anymore!

Ice Sprinkle

It's really a shame that today's children will never know some of the wonderful things that my generation experienced. Oh sure, they have electronic games, hi-tech toys, and all manner of plastic playthings – but they will never, for instance, know the thrill of an ice sprinkle on a sizzling summer day.

I can recall waiting with my playmates under a blistering sun for the ice delivery truck to come up Summer Street and turn into Wilder Street.

In a prominent window of each house, our mothers would have displayed a red cardboard sign with white numbers at each edge reading 5, 10, 15, and 20 on one side with higher numbers on the reverse. The sign would be turned so that the number of pounds of ice she wanted was displayed at the top. This saved the iceman from making two trips to her door. He would park as centrally as possible so that he could deliver to three or four houses without having to move his truck.

When the iceman opened the heavy canvas curtains at the back of the truck, we kids would gather round as he hacked at the ice with his pick. Chips would fly off, of course, and a dozen or more eager hands would reach to retrieve them. The idea was to have a mouth puffed full of ice chips and two fistfuls ready to pop into your mouth when you had room.

Since he carried the ice on his shoulder with tongs, the iceman wore a black rubber apron that ran from his chest, over his shoulders and down his back to below his belt. The bottom of this apron, in the back, had a deep pocket to collect melting ice so that it wouldn't drip on your mother's floor.

Advertisement, Athol Transcript, 1932

By the time he had serviced three or four houses and was ready to move his truck again, he had accumulated quite a lot of icy water in the apron pocket. This was when we would all crowd around him for an "ice sprinkle." He would tip one corner of his apron pocket and ice water would pour out the other side directly on our bare feet. Very few of us wore shoes in the summer and those who did "got barefoot" in a hurry when they heard the iceman coming. It wasn't really an ICE sprinkle, of course, it was a WATER sprinkle. But that water was just about as close to ice as it could get and still pour!

If there were a great number of kids, it was a knock-down drag-out getting in on an ice sprinkle. To get one foot chilled was doing OK, but to get both chilled was big league stuff.

I remember one summer a little kid named Fred came to visit with a family on Wilder Street. For two or three delivery days he stood and watched the crowd of us pushing and shoving and screaming as we fought for an ice sprinkle. Fred was just a litle guy about four or five, I guess, and he stood off to one side and watched with big, blue saucer eyes — too small and too intimidated to participate. The iceman began to feel sorry for Fred and one day he decided to make it up to him. Telling all the rest of us to stand aside, he went to the little boy and poured the entire contents of the apron pocket on his feet. The WHOLE thing!

Fred just stood there while the rest of us screamed our protests. Then his eyes welled up and tears began running down his cheeks in torrents as he stood, unmoving, in a puddle of ice water. The iceman's special gift, it seemed, had backfired. It had been too much for Fred. He had an accident in his pants.

The girl whose family Fred was visiting took him by the hand and led him quietly home — still sobbing silently while a whole apronful of ice water soaked slowly into the hot, dusty surface of Wilder Street.

It was a dark day in the life of the Wilder Street gang. But the ice sprinkles we got on the many other steaming days made up for it.

Local Heroes

We had a few local heroes too. I recall especially the Athol boxers of the thirties. Joe Gelinas, Charley Ersey, and Lefty Isrow come to mind — there may have been others. I never got to see any of them fight but, from the talk that went around at the time, apparently they were very promising prospects in the era of the Great Depression when many young men turned to boxing to make a few dollars. I saw Joe as a referee several times in later years — to my mind one of the best boxing officials in the country.

It was during this period that I gambled for the first time in my life. Joe Louis was scheduled to fight Jack Sharkey in the summer of 1936. Sharkey, whose real name was Joseph Zukauskas, was Lithuanian and, understandably, my Lithuanian friends were rooting for him. Louis had just been knocked out by Max Schmeling in 12 rounds and was not yet recognized as the devastating and superb fighter he really was. My Dad thought that Louis would win, though, and so I scraped together five pennies over the course of a few weeks (they were hard to come by in those days) and bet it all at 1-2 odds. When Louis KOed Sharkey in three rounds I suddenly found myself with 15 cents to spend. I went down to a drug store on Main Street and blew the whole pile on an extra large strawberry frappe. I guess I didn't look like I was worth 15 cents because the guy made me show my money before he made my frappe.

Another local hero I remember from the early thirties was aviator Bud Russell — Athol's answer to Charles Lindberg. He moved to Maine a few years later but he left a legacy of wild and hairy flying stories that may still be repeated around the Orange airport today. Most of them, I suspect, were expanded upon in their retelling and probably would have embarrassed Russell. I'm not sure if he ran the airport in some official capacity but he was certainly the premier pilot when the Orange airport was one of the busiest in that part of the state. I can barely remember flying with him in an old Curtiss Robin like the one Douglas "Wrong Way" Corrigan made headlines with in 1938. Corrigan took off from Brooklyn, N.Y., headed for Los Angeles but took a wrong turn somewhere and ended up in Dublin, Ireland. Seat-of-the-pants navigation never did become a science. To assist the other "Wrong Ways" of the air lanes, towns were required to paint a huge sign on the roof of a large building with the name, distance, and direction to the nearest airport in big orange letters with an arrow. It seems to me that the one in Orange was on the roof of the Minute Tapioca Co.

Like a lot of kids, I got the "flying bug" from hanging out with my dad at the Orange airport and attending the occasional airshows held there. Thanks to the GI Bill, I was able to realize my dream and learned to fly after World War II when Don Cookman and I enrolled at the Bowman Flying School in Keene, N.H. Don became a fine pilot but, as the saying goes, I learned just enough to be dangerous.

I recall with a combination of embarrassment and horror the night

Don Hager and I "cruised" Athol's Main Street in a Piper Cub. It was too dark for anyone to read our number so we wouldn't get caught, right? Wrong! The telephone lines to the airport were burning by the time we returned. As it happened, ours was the only plane up that night and we caught unshirted hell from everyone in authority at the airport when we landed.

For many of my childhood years, I dreamed of being a test pilot. I wanted to pull out of a "9-G dive" and bleed at the nose and ears like Clark Gable and Spencer Tracy in those 1930s aviation movies.

About the closest I ever came to a "9-G dive," however, was the day in 1947 when I taught Don Hager how to do a spin. (The blind leading the blind?) I gave him detailed instructions on how to enter a spin but only cursory mention of how to pull out. Up over North Orange somewhere, Don got the plane spinning in cracking good fashion and seemed to be enjoying himself immensely. After falling a couple thousand feet, however, I mentioned that perhaps we should stop spinning pretty soon before we ran out of air space. He reluctantly agreed and managed to get us out of the spin and into a howling dive.

"Well, what do I do now?" he asked grouchily, still somewhat piqued that we had to stop spinning.

"Pull back on the stick!" I shouted.

It was customary to do these things gradually and smoothly. I had neglected to brief Don on that aspect of flying, however, and with one mighty yank he pulled the stick all the way back.

That was the moment when I learned I would never have made a test pilot. My ears rang, my jowls sagged, and I was pinned in my seat. The poor little Piper Cub groaned in protest – it probably had never been treated that way before. I'm sure that old Mr. Piper never intended for his little plane to do that sort of thing.

I checked for signs of a nosebleed and asked Don to tell me if my ears showed signs of blood. None. Then I realized that if I had reached that state, the airplane very likely would be without wings. Those "9-G dives" were no longer the attraction they had been.

Don agreed, "Two G's maybe, but not nine. Let Clark Gable to do the bleeding."

For a future police safety officer, Hager didn't show a whole lot of safety consciousness in continuing to fly with me! One afternoon he wanted to photograph a bald eagle in flight. To accommodate him I

"Bud Russell — Athol's answer to Charles Lindbergh" (About 1928)

tried to "fly wing" on a beautiful specimen over the Quabbin Reservoir. It was due purely to luck, not flying ability, that we didn't end up in Millington or Enfield taking pictures of fish! I learned that an American bald eagle is infinitely more maneuverable than a Piper Cub. And bald eagles don't stall. Don got his pictures, though, and I have copies in my box of souvenirs.

Uncle Pete's Tales

Whenever I think of my "flying days," I remember my uncle, Pete Kingsbury, who was the world's greatest storyteller – at least in my world. He told the most exciting, zany, fascinating, and improbably outrageous tales I've ever heard. And this in an era in New England when storytelling was generally accorded the status of a fine art. There were a great many championship-class storytellers around the Athol area, but none could hold a candle to my Uncle Pete.

Someone once told him that he should join "Liars Anonymous." But he never really told lies – not the dirty, deceitful, dishonest kind. He told his wildly implausible tales purely for the entertainment value and to see just how far he could go before you caught on.

He always disguised his tales and never began a story with "Did I ever tell you about . . .?" That would have tipped you off to what was coming. Instead, it usually happened during a normal discussion when suddenly you would realize that the conversation had somehow taken a turn that led down the primrose path among the green pastures of Uncle Pete's fertile imagination. As you got older you learned to look for telltale signs – an inadvertent twinkle in his eye or a slight twitch at the corner of his mouth.

For years as an adolescent I thought he had led a most charmed life filled with miracles. I mean, who else could fall off a bridge, land in a hay truck passing beneath, and bounce from there into the lap of a beautiful blonde driving a robins-egg-blue Packard convertible?

Uncle Pete could convince you of almost anything. It's a good thing that he was a completely honest man. If he had put his talents to use in a criminal way he could have conned the Rockefellers out of most of their assets.

I remember one Christmas when I was about 9 or 10 I got one of those little engines that run on denatured alcohol. I was given explicit and repeated instructions and warnings about the lethality of the fuel. A couple days after Christmas, Uncle Pete dropped by and I proceeded to demonstrate my new toy. I left the room for a moment and when I returned Uncle Pete was just taking the bottle of alcohol from his lips. I shouted for him to not drink the stuff but he said it was too late — he had already swallowed a big swig of it. I was aghast and my dad gave the impression that he too was quite concerned.

Then Uncle Pete went into a death act that would have been the envy of Laurence Olivier. He gurgled, he choked, he gasped, his eyes bulged and he clutched his throat, his face reddened and his legs quivered. The final scene of "Titus Andronicus" is peaceful and sublime in comparison. Then just as he was panting his final words (I think it was the epitaph he wanted on his tombstone) my Aunt Evelyn came into the room and said "Oh, Pete! For heaven's sake, stop it!" Those were magic words. Uncle Pete was snatched from the brink just in the nick of time! He sheepishly explained to her that he was only trying to give me an object lesson.

Even as a child I sometimes doubted the truth of Uncle Pete's tales. But his stories were so delightfully entertaining that it was easy to forgive even massive lapses in veracity. So, perhaps he never really had a cow with three eyes that could hypnotize geese. And maybe that 6-foot catfish didn't really carry him to safety on the Mississippi when his steam-powered speed boat sank after being struck by lightning. But Dorothy didn't really go to the Land of Oz either.

The thing that made Uncle Pete's stories so captivating was that they were told as his personal experiences. He never made himself to be a hero, though. In his tales he was only a fascinated witness to what seemed to be a never-ending repertoire of everyday, run-of-the-mill miracles — an innocent bystander reluctantly drawn into hair-raising events that no one else in all the world would ever experience.

Years later, in 1947, when I passed my flight test and received my pilot's license, I was anxious to take somebody — anybody — for an airplane ride. It turned out that the next day (and apparently for the foreseeable future) everyone I knew had urgent things to attend to. In retrospect, I suppose that my reputation as the second or third worst driver in Worcester County was instinctively transferred to my flying ability. Anyway, only my Uncle Pete was ready and rarin' to be my first airplane passenger. Of course, after all the wild experiences he had told of surviving in his storybook life, flying with a brand new pilot carried no fear for him.

We went to the Keene airport, rented a Piper Cub, and had a grand afternoon. From that brief experience, I have no doubt that Uncle Pete found a kernel of fact upon which to build a dozen fantastic adventure stories. And, as I'm sure he intended, my confidence in my flying ability was given a much needed boost. Every boy should have an Uncle Pete.

Counting Cars

Each time I see an old car, my mind goes back to a game we played as children. On those sweltering summer afternoons when it was too darned hot to do anything physical, we would lie in the shade of a big tree alongside Route 32 and count the cars that passed. One kid would count all the GM cars, another all the Ford products, and a third all the Chrysler products. We would set a number, say 15 or 21, and the first one to reach it was the winner. If there was a fourth participant, he would take all the other makes of cars. We rarely saw a foreign car but there were plenty of "other" cars to make it competitive. There were the Hudson, Terraplane, Studebaker, Rockne, Graham, Nash, Lafayette, Auburn, Cord, Pierce Arrow, Franklin, Hupmobile, and Packard to name a few. Now, of course, all those cars have been replaced by Toyotas, Datsuns, VW's, Mazdas and the like.

Discovery and exploration are important pastimes of youth. I'm sure that most of us who grew up in the area north of Quabbin made many exciting "discoveries" as kids. Perhaps it was a small, half hidden cave where you could hide from marauding Indians, or a "secret" pool in a brook where you could go skinny dipping, or a special tree where, unseen among its branches, you could snipe quietly at passersby with your Winchester. I remember that way down at the very end of Green Street where the road peters out, and across the railroad tracks, there was the basement foundation of an old building, some rusted machinery, and the remnants of an old sluiceway. Since its abandonment, someone had covered over part of the basement with heavy metal plates to make, in effect, an underground hideout. Shrubs and trees had virtually obscured the area.

Clinton Fitch and I "discovered" the place one summer day in 1938 and immediately swore each other to secrecy. The place, we imagined, probably had been a gangster's hideout. We spent part of the next two or three days improving our secret clubhouse but, as with so many childhood endeavors, we quickly grew tired of it and found other things to occupy our time. Sometime later I broke my vow of secrecy and confided our discovery to my Dad. He laughed and told me that he and his pals had also "discovered" that place when he was a boy. He thought it had once been a laundry back around the turn of the century. He said he doubted that any gangsters had ever used it but, seeing my disappointment, conceded that they might have. That place is probably still there today and undoubtedly has been "discovered" by countless other Athol youngsters through the years.

Tarzanland

Across the river from that spot, and upstream a ways, is a strange area that seems out of place with the general Millers River environment. It is not a big area but it is covered with a dense growth of vines and brambles virtually to the water's edge. We called it "Tarzanland" although the foliage was so dense that you couldn't really swing from tree to tree on the vines. I lived on Chestnut Hill Avenue when I was about 9 or 10 and it was an easy hike down to Tarzanland. My mother often made me a sack lunch and my dog Major and I would spend the day fishing and exploring the river. With a pair of my Dad's snips I had cut a low crawlway into Tarzanland and fashioned a couple of "secret chambers" deep in the vines. The "chambers" were interconnected with almost invisible crawlways. In the heat of the early afternoon, Major and I would retreat into the cool leafy area to rest and eat our lunch. It was an idyllic spot with the sun barely filtering through the vines and the sound of the close-by but unseen river. It was a place to dream and let your imagination soar. You could hear the sounds of native drums, or a tramp riverboat chugging upstream, or a Pan Am Clipper taking off for some strange and distant destination. Safaris left hourly for exotic places like Timbuktoo or the upper Nile. In later years I would really travel to many distant and exotic parts of the world. But the real places were always a disappointment compared to those I dreamed of there in Tarzanland at the edge of the Millers River.

My Dog Major

Many of the childhood images I carry in my memory are like something out of a Norman Rockwell painting. A-boy-and-his-dog was frequently a Rockwell theme and I easily identify with that nostalgic vision.

My dog Major was an almost constant companion for several years of my life. An uncle had found him stunned and half frozen beside a road in Wendell. After nursing him back to health, my uncle gave him to me on my birthday in November, 1936. He was fully grown when he came to me (we estimated his age to be about 3 or 4 years) and we decided that he was part mastiff and part German shepherd. I don't remember who named him.

Major was a fairly big dog. He was colored dark brown and black on his head, back and sides, fading to tan on his chest, underside and legs. He had a tremendous bark, roughly equivalent to the sound of a 120mm howitzer. He was a wonderful watchdog mainly because of his resounding voice and fierce appearance. Actually, he was the gentlest and most trustworthy of dogs.

In his own canine world, Major was extremely macho and was instantly ready for battle when any male dog came into his view. Being a very obedient dog, as a rule, saved him from many potentially vicious dog fights. However, his obedience to man waned in the presence of amorous lady dogs. He had an apparently insatiable sexual appetite and a complete lack of modesty and decorum in that regard.

I had a magazine delivery route for a couple of years in the late '30s (Saturday Evening Post, Ladies Home Journal, Country Gentleman, and Liberty) and Major accompanied me every step of the way in fair weather or foul. We explored the Millers River together on many a summer day, walked in the snow in the woods together in winter, and during vacation from school went skinny-dipping together in out-of-the-way water holes.

The years passed and I became increasingly interested in girls and cars and things to do away from home. I saw Major every day, of course, but our shared, special times together became less and less frequent. He grew older, touches of gray appeared around his nose and chest, and he relied more and more on my mother's offerings rather than the fruits of his own hunting.

In the spring of 1944, I came home from work one evening to find the family unusually somber. My dad took me aside and told me the sad news — Major was dead. He had passed away quietly in his sleep in his "room" in the shed attached to the house. My mother had gone out to bring him food and he did not respond.

Dad thought it would be too much of an ordeal for me to have to bury Major so he had dug a grave at the end of the garden just where the woods began. He placed Major in the grave and left it open so I could see him one last time.

It was getting dark as I took a kerosene lantern and went out to the grave. Dad had arranged Major so that he appeared to be sleeping with his chin on his paws — his usual position of repose.

I put down the lantern, knelt beside the grave, and reached down and patted that massive old head. I told him I was sorry that I hadn't spent as much time with him over the past few years as I should have. I talked about all the many happy times we had shared. I recalled the time he scared "Corky," the Fuller Brush Man's cockatoo, into spouting obscenities — up to that time, as far as we knew, Corky's only words were "Hello, Corky" and "Goodbye, Corky." I think I ex-

plained to Major that I had often thought of buying him a great big steak for his birthday but then had realized I didn't know his birthday. However, the butcher at the uptown A&P had occasionally given me massive bones for Major — one or two were, I think, from the hind leg of a brontosaurus. How Major did strut with a massive bone in his teeth!

I irrelevantly explained to my old pal that I would be leaving for the Navy in a few weeks and so we would have been apart for a long time anyway. It would have been nice, though, to think of Major being a part of my eventual homecoming.

I don't know how long I talked to Major and petted him, but much later I heard my dad coming up the garden. He stopped a few feet from me. He had a shovel.

Dad stood silent for a few minutes and then he said, "Your supper's getting cold, Son. Don't you think you'd better go in?"

I nodded and stood up.

Major's highest compliment was to call him a "GOOD dog." Other phrases like "great dog" or "wonderful dog" or anything else were not understood. But tell him he was a "GOOD dog" and his tail would wag so hard it about threw his back out of joint. He always seemed to beam and glow at those words. It seemed so late and so inadequate now but it was what he would have understood best.

"He was a GOOD dog, Dad," I said through my tears.

Then I went back to the house. My dad took care of the necessary remaining chore.

Dogs were never the bother that they often seem to be today. For instance nobody I knew ever took their dog in for a haircut and shampoo. And no one was going to provide his dog with a sweater when he couldn't afford one for himself. Unless it was a hunting dog, about all you ever asked of a pooch was to do his duty on someone else's lawn and chew the socks off salesmen and bill collectors. In the process, a dog became a member of the family — a loyal friend and constant companion that a boy would remember all the days of his life.

Chapter 2

'It Shall Not Be Again'

I suppose an important aspect of growing up is the inevitable awareness of one's sexuality. It's a sticky problem that every adolescent has to cope with sooner or later. Nowadays, with the proliferation of readily accessible books and magazines and even school courses on the subject, I guess the average kid passes quickly through the "birds-'n'-bees" stage — or skips over it entirely. In 1930s New England, though, sexual awareness was terribly slow in development and nearly always baffling. No one talked openly about "it." Any pearls of sexual wisdom were whispered (among the boys at least) on a remote corner of the Highland School playground during recess or any other place where you wouldn't be overheard by an adult. The very people who had all the information about this puzzling subject — the adults — kept it all to themselves. If you mustered enough nerve to ask a sensitive question, you often got a cuff on the ear as a reply. Or, you were sent to your room to forget about such bad things. Concentrated forgetting never did work, of course, but you were expected to try.

As a consequence, what we got was distorted (often alarming) descriptions and explanations that had been passed for the umpteenth time from unknowing mouths to innocent ears. It's a good thing the sex urge is as strong as it is. Otherwise, on the basis of the startling information we passed along, most of us would gladly have chosen a life of celibacy.

But the urge is strong and we all succumb to a compelling curiousity at some point in our adolescence. I remember that Tully Brook has several wide pools, each with a number — First Tully, Second Tully, and so on. One of the "Tullys" (I've forgotten which one) was supposedly reserved for girls only, and, so the wiseacres told you, the girls went skinny-dipping there. I wonder how many fruitless and futile hours overly-curious Athol boys spent lurking in the bushes above that spot waiting for the "village belles to peel!" It may have been the single most observed spot in Worcester County. Well, if our curiosity was unsatisfied, at least it kept us off the streets.

My introduction to "it" came rather unexpectedly. One summer afternoon when I was about 9 or 10, I was eating my sack lunch in my secret "chamber" in Tarzanland. Major was off trying to roust out his own lunch of woodchuck or rabbit when along came a young couple at the river's edge. To my surprise, instead of continuing on they paused and searched out the entryway that Major and I used. They crawled inside the underbrush to the first "chamber" and for a panicky moment or two I thought I would be discovered. I sat frozen in my second "inner chamber" while only 15 or 20 feet away they began "carrying on," as the expression was in those days. I could barely see them through the thick vines and underbrush that separated our two chambers and their conversation was somewhat muffled and mostly unintelligible.

After some moments, Major returned from an unsuccessful search for food and crawled through the entryway into the first chamber where our uninvited guests were making themselves at home. Major was a gregarious and fun-loving pooch and enjoyed nothing more than a good ol' fashioned wrestling match (he always joined in with me and my brothers at home). With open good nature he launched himself into the fray. Upon Major's arrival and unsought participation, however, the poignancy of the moment was abruptly shattered for the couple, and, amid shrieks and screams and curses, they fled distraught and disheveled out to the water's edge. Major was left panting wistfully and wagging his tail in apparent disappointment. And I was left to ponder new emotions and baffling questions that would remain unanswered for several more years.

Movies

It's sort of strange in this age of television and home video to think of a movie theater as a significant feature of life. Yet, the York and Capitol theaters in Athol have an important place in my memory. The Capitol, as I recall, seemed to feature "B" movies like those awful Republic flicks featuring somebody named Vera Hruba Ralston whose only claim to continued starring roles was that her husband owned the studio. Saturday matinees at the Capitol always drew a large crowd of kids, however, for such serialized adventure stories as Flash Gordon with Buster Crabbe, or Winslow of the Navy, or Renfrew of the Mounties. Buck Jones, Tom Mix, Hopalong Cassidy, and the Lone Ranger were all serialized westerns, at one time or another, and there were numerous cartoons including Felix the Cat and Betty Boop. For years, as I recall, the price was only a nickel for Saturday matinees.

The York, though, was a different story. I always had the impression that the York was pretty classy. The long blue carpeted corridor from the ticket booth to the foyer with its framed billboards announc-

Photo Dick Chaisson Collection

York Theater on Main Street in Athol, 1934

ing coming attractions, the large foyer with its gold-framed mirrors and cushioned bench seats, and the carpeted double stairway leading to the balcony entrances — all these things seemed to suggest affluence and sophistication in those years of the Great Depression.

I wonder how many Athol couples of my generation had as their "first date" a movie at the York. It could be expensive if you were really trying to impress your date. With theater tickets, goodies to nibble on, and a late bite after the show at Carbone's restaurant next door a guy could blow close to two dollars in an evening!

Until about the late '30s, the York included vaudeville in the program from time to time. I can remember the marquee reading something like: "Jeannette MacDonald and Nelson Eddy in 'Rosalie' Plus 3 Acts of Vaudeville." They say that vaudeville in America died a slow painful death and I think it had its last final agonies at the York. For a while the theaters offered free dishes with each ticket to entice Atholians to attend. I recall, too, the marquee reading "15 Degrees Cooler Inside," and on a blistering summer afternoon that was a real enticement. Come to think of it, the York may have been the only air-conditioned building in town.

The first movies that I remember seeing (it must have been about 1933 or so) were in Orange when they were shown at the town hall. Disney's "Three Little Pigs" and "The Invisible Man" were two I distinctly recall – the first because it was so enchanting to a second-grader and the latter because it scared the daylights out of me. I fairly flew home that night with an imaginary invisible man dogging my every step. Orange finally got a real theater after World War II and the opening show was, as I recall, "The Jolson Story," with Larry Parks and Evelyn Keyes.

I remember that there were other forms of entertainment in the area from time to time. For a few years in the late '30s they ran motorcycle races at the fairgrounds during the summer. And one summer, it must have been 1941, a carnival came to town that billed itself as the largest in the world. It took up the whole fairground. There were rides and games and cotton candy but the thing I remember most is the girlie show.

The star performer was a buxom redhead who performed with four tassles attached – two fore and two aft. With astounding muscle control and eye-popping gyrations, she could get all four tassles whirling at once like some exquisitely designed B-17. She was the talk of high

Photo Dick Chaisson Collection

Fairgrounds during Athol bicentennial pageant, September 1935

school locker rooms for the first several weeks of the new school year. There were occasional smaller carnivals that used to set up in a small open area off Freedom Street, but none featured acts like the multi-engined redhead at the fairgrounds.

I remember a guy who came to town one time billed as "human fly." Quite a crowd gathered one night as, in a spotlight, he climbed the face of the Leonard Hotel. There was a smattering of applause as he waved from the hotel roof but by-and-large I have the recollection that most people were not overly impressed. With typical Yankee disdain for the frivolous, most people thought him a bit loony. I remember my dad muttering, "A grown man ought to be able to find something better than that to do for a living!" As a PR stunt the affair was a dud.

Sometime in the mid '30s, it was announced that the first "streamlined" train would be coming through the local towns. It was called the "Flying Yankee," I think. My grandfather took me down to the depot in Orange to witness the event. It passed very slowly through the station and did not stop. It had been advertised as being capable of speeds in excess of 100 miles per hour, and I remember being upset that it didn't go rocketing by at full throttle.

Johnny Johnstone and the YMCA

The YMCA must surely have been the hub of activity for Athol boys since the day it was built. I'll bet every boy who ever lived in Athol has fond memories of that place. For all the years that I enjoyed its facilities, Johnny Johnstone was the director.

In later years when I had three boisterous sons of my own, I remembered Johnny and his unrivaled ability to handle boys. The man was an absolute marvel. I never saw him angry. He maintained order and discipline in the most benign way. He was at once a leader, a friend and confidante, an instructor, an organizer, a motivator, an arbitrator. If ever there was a perfect match of man and job it was Johnny Johnstone and the directorship of the Athol YMCA.

I can recall racing down from Riverbend School during the noon hour for a quick dip in the YMCA pool. We nearly always tarried too long and arrived back late and sweaty for the afternoon class. It was a challenge to come up with a different excuse each time we were late. We were reluctant to confess where we had been for fear that someone would make a rule and shut down that activity.

Sometime in the late '30s, Johnny Johnstone formed a new YMCA club called the Friendly Indians. It was designed, I think, for us kids in town who could not afford the uniforms and other expensive paraphernalia required by the Boy Scouts. The only regalia we had was a cloth Indian head which your mother could sew on your sweater or jacket. The dues were a nickel a month — just so we could feel we were paying our own way, I guess. We participated in lots of YMCA activities, including the annual hatchet hunt, and occasionally went on one-day hikes. Some of us had hand-me-down or borrowed knapsacks and canteens but most of us carried our lunch in a paper sack and our beverage in a glass canning jar. We were supposed to wear our Indian head insignia but I remember that my mother had sewn mine on my good sweater which she wouldn't let me wear to go hiking.

Memorial Day in Athol

I suppose that holidays are among the best remembered times in our lives. Memorial Day in Athol is a vivid memory of my childhood. Quite in contrast to the recent decade or two of anti-military feelings in this country, during the '30s the parades with their flags, uniforms, and bands were greeted with considerable patriotic fervor. The World War I veterans made up the largest contingent, and there were still a half dozen or so Spanish-American War veterans who marched.

Until the mid '30s there were also two Civil War veterans who rode in an open car to the ceremonies at the uptown common. Still not fully understanding the process of aging, I can remember being disappointed at their appearance. They were somewhat infirm and wore civilian clothes. Their only military regalia was their broad-brimmed black hats and a couple of medals pinned to their lapels. It was difficult for a child to associate those aged men with the young soldiers of Gettysburg and Antietam pictured in our school textbooks. I think today how wonderful it would have been to talk to them and hear first hand accounts of the Battle of Bull Run or Petersburg.

Fort Devens always sent a small contingent of active duty soldiers to Athol's Memorial Day ceremonies. They were the object of tittering attention by teenage nymphets and of envy and frustration by teenage boys. For us younger boys, however, the ultimate thrill of the day was to strut along in step with the marching soldiers as if some of the glamor of their uniforms and military bearing would rub off on us. At the ceremony, we all watched one another to see who might flinch when the soldiers fired a salute.

For all the genuine respect paid the military men, both veterans and active duty, the underlying theme of all the speeches was a determination that America would never go to war again. I suppose some of the adults still believed that World War I, "the war to end war," had indeed been successful in that regard. Few were paying much attention to the mustachioed madman in Berlin or the strutting martinet in Rome.

I was at the dedication of the statue in the little park in Orange, across from the fire station. Expecting a heroically postured soldier depicted in the heat of battle, my childish concepts were disappointed when the statue was unveiled.

Years later when I returned from World War II, I saw that memorial in a different light. Today I think of it as the most poignant war memorial I've ever seen, with its inscription "It Shall Not Be Again." The child depicted on the statue probably would have the same unknowing disappointment that I felt at the unveiling. But with maturity he would, like his father, deplore war and its inhumanities. He would serve his country in its extreme danger but would return with his father's determination — "It shall not be again!"

So it goes through history. When will the father's view prevail?

Teachers

I think too few of us realize during our school years the impact and influence our teachers have on our lives.

Quite apart from their purely curricular purpose, they influence our moral development, our self-discipline, our motivation and many other facets of our emerging character. As a so-so student I never felt a close affinity to my teachers. It was only with the passage of years that I began to see them from a different perspective. I recognize now how deeply most of them cared for my welfare and future well-being. I remember their acts of kindness and I also remember what at the time I considered their acts of tyranny. From an adult point of view, however, I can make a detached judgment of my disciplinary cases — "it served him right!"

I think the most effective disciplinary system of any school I ever attended was that at the Lake Park School. If it was decided that an offending student was deserving of maximum punishment — a razor strap applied liberally to the palm of an outstretched hand — the student had to fetch the strap. Mrs. Ray was the custodian of the strap which meant that you had to enter her classroom and (before her class of snickering sixth-graders) ask in a loud clear voice, "Mrs. Ray — may I please have the strap?!"

If you mumbled, you had to repeat the request. Mrs. Ray would then hand you the strap and you had to report to the office of the principal (Mrs. Pollard) where the sentence was carried out by your teacher (Miss Ryan, in my case). Then came the worst part of all — you had to return the strap to Mrs. Ray, tear-stained cheeks, reddened eyes and all in full view of those damned sixth-graders. To my mind the Spanish Inquisition would have been an appealing alternative. I really looked forward to the day when I would graduate to the sixth grade and have my turn at snickering.

My family moved uptown, however, and I attended the sixth grade in Miss Eva Bonnette's class at Highland School. (I cannot recall any corporal punishment at the Highland School.) The Spanish Civil War was going on at the time and I remember Miss Bonnette's deep concern about the destruction caused by the fighting. Her dream was to someday visit Spain and tour the famous old cities, castles and museums. Each time I visited Spain in later years I recalled her glowing descriptions that fired our imaginations as sixth-graders. It is as beautiful as she described. I hope sincerely that Miss Bonnette one day got to see her castles in Spain.

At the Riverbend School the next year I had Mr. Emory Hastings for homeroom in the seventh grade. Among other subjects, Mr. Hastings taught a course in music appreciation. He had a wonderful record collection of the classics which he played for us as he interpreted the meanings and movements of the great masters. I can think of few less rewarding tasks than that of trying to cram culture into unreceptive minds. To this day, however, I recall his obvious enthusiasm for his subject.

On the last day of the course he gave us the opportunity to select any one of the records to replay. Almost unanimously, I recall, the class shouted that they wanted to hear "the Lone Ranger song." Good and wise educator that he was, he probably anticipated that. I've wished many times since, though, that ours had been the one class to request Mozart's 25th Symphony, or Rimsky-Korsakov's "Scheherazade," or Beethoven's "Appassionata." It would have made his year!

I remember other teachers at Riverbend School, too. There was Miss Kumin and Miss Petrosky, Miss Fitzgibbons (the "Blonde Bombshell" – a stern disciplinarian), good natured and affable Mr. Joe Gagliardi, and the principal, Mr. Taylor.

I remember one day Albine Piragis and I were sent to Mr. Taylor's office for an infraction of some rule or other. My father had once told me that he had had Mr. Taylor for a teacher and, seeking to alleviate

Photo Dick Chaisson Collection

Highland School, built in 1899, was closed in 1966, demolished in 1983

the situation somewhat, I mentioned that my dad was a former student of his. Bad choice! That was when I learned for the first time that my dad had been something less than a model student. I don't recall that Albine and I suffered any more for my indiscretion but it was an eye opener for me to learn that my strict disciplinarian father had been somewhat of a hellion as a kid!

Petersham High

My family moved again, and in 1940 I entered Petersham High School. Mr. Philip Arnold was the school principal at the time and he and I never quite saw eye to eye on anything. Always the impeccably attired academician, he had, nonetheless, beneath his quiet demeanor, an aura of latent explosiveness. I always had the impression that his first instinct was to do me grievous bodily harm and his second instinct was to get me out of his sight.

Thankfully he always curbed the first (if it was really there at all). He did, however, get me out of his sight on at least two occasions — once when he kicked me off the basketball team and once he kicked me out of school. On both occasions, though, he quickly relented and reinstated me, but our limited relationship was never cordial and more often than not took the form of a confrontation.

I avoided him as much as possible and even dropped all his classes. Mr. Arnold taught the math and science courses at PHS and by avoiding him I had an awful lot of making up to do years later when I studied algebra, trig, and physics during my meteorology courses in the Navy. I was quite successful in avoiding Mr. Arnold, which was a real accomplishment in a school with only 50 or so students. Sometimes weeks would go by without a face-to-face meeting. On those rare occasions when we met he would stare at me with a puzzled look as though wondering where he had seen me before. As his recognition of me returned, however, that terrible smoldering glare would come into his eyes. I would then exit as gracefully as my overwhelming panic would permit and try not to run into him again for another semester.

My fear of Mr. Arnold notwithstanding, I enjoyed Petersham High School immensely. I recall my classmates and teachers with great affection. I have thought many times through the years how very fortunate I was to be able to attend that small high school where "everybody knew everybody." Without exception my classmates were decent, honest, friendly, caring teenagers — the kind you wish your children could attend school with. Not that we were all angels by any means. But there was an abiding concern for the property of others, a respect for authority, a general compliance with rules, and a concern (not always rigidly observed) for standards of conduct.

One of my favorite teachers at PHS was Miss Amsden, a petite lady who looked as though she had just stepped out of the 19th century. Miss Amsden taught the art courses and, having a certain amount of art talent, I did well in her classes.

One of my most embarrassing moments happened in Miss Amsden's art class in my sophomore year. One afternoon I was seated at a table next to my pretty classmate Barbara Bryant, in whom I had an abiding interest at the time. I got up to sharpen a pencil or get supplies or something and, when I returned, Paul Radasch had moved my drawing board down the table and he was seated in the place next to Barbara.

With the limited civility macho teenagers have in such situations, I told him that he was on my stool and asked him to move. With equal civility he told me what I could do with my stool. In a moment of unthinking reaction I grabbed him by the collar and belt, pulled him off the stool, and threw him toward the middle of the room just as Miss Amsden arrived to see what the commotion was about. Stumbling backwards, Paul crashed into our teacher and down the two of them went with arms, legs, and Miss Amsden's skirts flying.

I was absolutely horrified. I couldn't move. Barbara, however, went immediately to Miss Amsden's assistance and, thank heaven, she was unhurt. Ordinarily, Paul would have responded to such a challenge by coming off the floor prepared to commit mayhem. But Paul knew how to make the most out of a golden opportunity. He jumped to his feet shouting "He did it! He did it!" while waving an accusing finger under my nose. I wanted to bite it off but I figured I was in enough hot water as it was.

Miss Amsden, a most gracious and understanding lady, never reprimanded me or sent me to see Mr. Arnold (which is what I feared most). I didn't get off scot-free, however. She banished me to the isolation of an alcove — a sort of penalty box — for a couple of weeks. And Barbara didn't speak to me for a month!

It was an awfully embarrassing moment but I think the most humiliating aspect came a couple of weeks later. The Center School in

Petersham contained all grades from one through twelve. One day I overheard a second or third grader telling another as he pointed to me from behind a bush, "There goes that tall skinny guy that beat the hell outta Miss Amsden!" They never let you live it down!

Another favorite teacher was Miss Semple who taught English and literature. It was she who first noticed in me a germ of writing ability. She encouraged my writing talents and, with marginal results, crammed a certain amount of grammar into my head. Her praise and extra attention to my latent skills provided my first motivation toward the profession in which I was to earn a good living in later years.

About ten years ago my brother Norm and I spent about 48 hours in the old home area and a visit to the lovely old Center School in Petersham was a "must." We arrived just after school had let out for the day, but John LePoer invited us in to tour the place. He then requested that we autograph the books we had written (the school had purchased the entire "People of Destiny" set). I have attended interviews, author's days, press conferences, and autograph parties but none could approach the satisfaction I received from sitting at my old desk in my old school autographing my books. Miss Semple would have been proud!

Joining The Work Force

By my 16th birthday I was convinced that I knew just about anything there was to know about everything with the possible exception of brain surgery, international banking, and one or two other fields that I did not intend to pursue anyway. So I quit high school and set out to make my million.

I got off to a rousing start when I was hired by Matt Meany in the UTD shipping room at a starting wage of 37½ cents an hour. After a training period of a month or so, we were supposed to get a raise. It wasn't automatic, however. You had to ask for it. I was terribly nervous about facing the very stern Mr. Meany and a week or more passed beyond my eligibility date for a raise. I finally came up with a great idea. One morning I followed him into the men's room, waited until I was sure he was comfortably situated, and then made my well rehearsed pitch to his shoes and pants cuffs — all that showed beneath the stall door. He was a bit startled, I suspect, but heard my request and assured me that I would get a raise in my next pay envelope. I thanked him and bolted out the door even before he had a chance to pull the chain. The raise brought my wage to 40 cents an hour and I was delighted. My dad was also impressed.

"Well, Son," he said approvingly, "Now you're making as much money as a man!"

The job at the UTD was actually my second job. I had worked summers during high school for Mr. Horace Coolidge on his farm in Petersham. Mr. Coolidge was a gentle giant of a man. Perhaps my memory exaggerates a little but I have the impression that he must have weighed a powerful 260 pounds or more and was six feet, four or five inches tall. He played a musical instrument in the town band, and at concerts when he tapped his foot to the music the bass drum became superfluous. The bandstand shook and the ground trembled. Some people said that the side of the Petersham bandstand where Mr. Coolidge sat was several inches lower — having been gradually pounded down through the years as he kept time to the music.

Mr. Coolidge was a well-educated man (University of Maine, as I recall), and why he chose to be a farmer I'll never know. I guess he was a man motivated to hard physical labor. He always did far more work than any of his hired hands. Years later in researching my book on Frank Lloyd Wright, I discovered that Wright had worked on an uncle's farm as a boy. His description of the never-ceasing, back-breaking toil ("adding tired to tired" is the way Wright put it) brought back memories for me of Mr. Coolidge's farm. To choose farming as a way of life must be a mystical calling that some people can't resist. I remember those long, hot summers with a sense of pride. It was a personal test, to work on a New England farm. I'm glad I had the opportunity. And I'm glad that I was fortunate enough to work for a man like Mr. Coolidge.

Of all the difficult jobs on a farm, I think that mowing away hay in a loft is the most miserable. Bumps Barnes and I were invariably assigned that job by Mr. Coolidge. The temperature in a hayloft in August somewhat approximates that of at least the outskirts of Hades. The air is filled with chaff that gravitates to a sweating body like metal filings to a magnet. Because we wore only shorts, sneakers, and a straw hat, Bumps and I emerged from the barn completely chaff-covered and looking like fuzzy stick figures. Just to be able to breathe again was reward in itself but Mrs. Coolidge turned the moment into an ultimate pleasure — the last-day-of-school and discharge-from-the-Army rolled into one. First she hosed us off with water that I am convinced was piped in directly from the polar ice cap. This sent us into fits and contortions that very closely resembled the "break dancing" that is the current rage in the country. When we had calmed down, she served us homemade cookies and all the ice cold fresh milk we could drink. After the last load of the day she had a special treat for us, like strawberries and cream or strawberry shortcake and lemonade. I remember sitting on a stone wall near the barn absolutely exhausted but no longer itching from the chaff and with my temperature returning to normal, while consuming those wonderful offerings and thinking "this is just about as close as I'll ever get to heaven."

Dad's Packard 'Truck'

As with most rural boys of that era, I learned to drive at a very early age. I had hardly got started, at age 13, when I had my first accident. I bounced over the curb in my dad's Packard truck and ran smack dab into Mr. Ross' barber shop. I think that barber shop was located next to where Bruce's Pharmacy is now (it is a restaurant at present, I think). Thank heaven no one was walking along that stretch of sidewalk at that particular moment. My dad wasn't even in the car with me.

Fortunately, the barber shop had a pretty solid base under the window. Little damage was done to anything except Mr. Ross' good nature. He was really fuming at me when my dad arrived. And that's what saved me from severe punishment. My dad could discipline his children with vigor and finesse but he reserved that right to himself alone (with limited franchise to school teachers and law enforcement agencies).

He got between me and the highly irate Mr. Ross and soon I had Dad's total sympathy while the unfortunate barber faced Dad's steadily rising wrath. It was all worked out in due time and in a civilized fashion. The police were never involved, but the affair made an inauspicious beginning to my driving record.

Even those old enough to remember the fine and elegant Packard automobile have probably never heard of a Packard truck. The one my dad had obviously was a hybrid. In 1939, he bought a 1928 Packard sedan, cut it off behind the front seat, put a truck body on it and went into the hauling business. We could not afford a car during the Great Depression but a truck would pay for itself in the long run.

My Dad and the Packard "truck" (about 1940)

Dad arranged to buy wood on the stump (that had been downed by the hurricane of 1938) from Harvard Forest for fifty cents per cord. We cut it into four-foot lengths and sold it in Athol for five dollars per cord. Dad also hauled chicken manure and coal ashes. He always arranged to have a customer on the other end who needed manure for a garden or cinders for a driveway and so he got paid twice for the same job. He never got rich, but his hard work (he maintained a full-time job in Starrett's) and ingenuity kept our family nose above the Depression waters.

The old Packard finally gave out after about a year of heavy use. Dad junked the Packard, kept the truck body and attached it to a 1933 V-12 Cadillac limousine he bought. As with the Packard, Dad cut the Cadillac off behind the front seat and mounted the truck body. It may have been the only twelve-cylinder truck in the state. It would, my dad said, "pass anything on the road except a gas station."

Dad always liked big, powerful cars. At the time of his death in 1979 he owned a monstrous black Lincoln sedan with automatic everything. I have just a suspicion that somewhere in the back of his mind he sheltered a latent instinct to cut that thing in half and make a truck out of it.

Chapter 3

'Make It Do Or Do Without'

The human brain is a wonderful thing. It's like a computer where information is collated and merged and stored for future retrieval. In the course of time, unused or trivial information is usually dropped from memory but every now and then some insignificant bits of data get permanently stored and forgotten only to be unexpectedly retrieved years later. Take songs for example. Some unsuspected impulse pushes your "retrieve" button when you least expect it and suddenly you're whistling or singing songs you haven't thought of in 50 years.

One night a few months ago my wife and I were having dinner in a restaurant in Carmel when, during a pause in the conversation, I suddenly sang:

"Shave and a haircut, two bits!
Who did you marry? Tom Mix!
How did you like him? Okay!"

My wife stared at me with some apprehension. "Is that your second glass of wine?" she asked suspiciously.

"No! No! No!" I protested. "It's not the wine. I just suddenly remembered a ditty we used to sing as kids in Athol."

"What made you think of that?" she asked.

"I don't know," I replied, as puzzled as she was.

"What do the words mean?" she asked.

"Nothing, I guess. They don't have to mean anything, it's just a kid's song."

My wife stared at me for a long moment. "You've been working too hard," she said finally, in a voice heavy with compassion. "Why don't we take a vacation."

The binary bits and bytes of my brain were still on "retrieve," however, and suddenly I found myself singing:

"Oh, there was an old man and he had a wooden leg.
He didn't have no money and he didn't wanna beg.
So he took two spools and an old tin can,
And he made himself a Ford and the darn thing ran."

"Another Athol song?" my wife asked, as she smiled reassurance at the increasingly nervous maitre d'.

"Yeah!" I said with growing appreciation and amazement at the things I still had stored from childhood. "Didn't you have songs like that when you were a kid here in California? How about "Fido is a Hot Dog Now?"

"Why don't we skip dessert tonight," she suggested, nicely evading my question. "You can sing about Fido to me on the way home."

As he returned my credit card, the waiter said he'd love to hear "When Willie Wet the Bed" but he had other tables to wait on. The maitre d' respectfully declined to listen to a couple of choruses of "Fargo Fanny." "Perhaps some other time, Monsieur!"

It's a shame. Here I have all these songs and ditties from my childhood on instant retrieval and no one wants to listen. They conjure up for me, warm recollections of childhood that are locked forever in a moment of my life that is perhaps unshareable with strangers.

It's odd that no matter how many times you hear a song over the years, many are set to a specific time or event in your memory. Each time I hear Irving Berlin's "Easter Parade," for example, I am taken back to Easter of 1936 when my family and all my cousins, uncles, and aunts spent a fabulous weekend at an uncle's camp on a small stream near Wendell Depot. Another song, "Elmer's Tune," always reminds me of the basketball season of 1941 and of all of us singing on the Petersham School bus that carried us to "away" games. Surely we must have sung other songs on those trips but only "Elmer's Tune" brings back the memory for me. The song "Marie" always reminds me of a girl by that name who rode Mr. Mann's old Reo school bus for a while when I was in seventh grade. The song was a big hit for Tommy Dorsey at the time and this girl was a big hit with me. I was absolutely infatuated with her. She was an older woman, however (she must have been 16 or 17), and she didn't even know I existed. Today I can't even remember what she looked like, but memories of boyhood frustration return each time I hear "Marie."

Other words that spring to mind when you least expect it are the axioms, mottos, golden rules, proverbs, dictums and commandments by which we were supposed to live our lives. We were bombarded with them. "Waste not, want not," "Neither a borrower nor lender be," and "The squeaking wheel gets the grease" are examples.

There seemed to be an appropriate phrase for every action in our lives. Some seemed to contradict others, however. If you tried to live by the rules you ran into such problems as choosing between "Look before you leap" and "He who hesitates is lost."

I think the one I like most, though, is:

"Use it up, wear it out;
Make it do, or do without!"

Now that to me represents the bluntness and taciturn economy of words that most people associate with New Englanders. It also reflects the thrift, frugality, and no-nonsense approach to life that I remember from the Depression years.

'Village Idiots'

We had a couple of local characters that remain in my memory from those Depression years. Each was referred to at times as the "village idiot" – an expression I haven't heard since I left New England. One was called "Weary Willie" and the other "Crazy Tom."

I never did get to know Weary Willie. He was a quiet little man. He always wore a floppy old broad-brimmed hat – it looked like one of John Wayne's Stetsons that had sat out on a fence post through too many thundershowers. He could be seen almost anywhere in town at any time of the day or night pulling a wobbly old cart. I suppose he collected junk. Willie always seemed to have a destination in mind. He never looked to right or left and was very deliberate about his movements. He never ran, but he never tarried, and I think I never heard him speak. Also, Willie never looked you in the eye. He looked over you, under you, around you, and through you but never at you. When I first moved to Athol, a third-grade classmate at Main Street School told me that if Willie ever did look you right in the eye, all your hair would fall out. Since I didn't have any bald classmates, I assumed that everyone was being very careful around Weary Willie.

Crazy Tom was just the opposite of Weary Willie in many respects. Willie was industrious, purposeful, and withdrawn. Tom was noisy, babbled incessantly and wandered around uptown with no apparent purpose. Older boys often teased Tom and worked him into a bit of a tizzy but he was not a violent person.

He loved to talk and would follow you half way home or to school trying to inspire and maintain a conversation. His mind was like a cluttered attic where he kept the assorted and unrelated bits of information he had accumulated over 50 years or so. He was always a very attentive listener and seemed grateful whenever anyone would bother to pause and speak to him.

Having a conversation with Tom, however, was an exercise in futility. If he met you on the sidewalk he would usually greet you with, "Hey. Where ya off to?"

"Well, Tom," you might reply, "I'm going over to Grace Pitts' store for some thread for my mother and then to Bemis' for a loaf of bread."

There would be a pause while Tom rummaged around in the murky recesses of his memory for an appropriate response. His eyes would roll around as if trying to turn inward to read the message he was about to impart.

"Warren G. Harding has white hair," he would finally state with conviction. "He went to Alaska to die. He lives in San Francisco now."

Once you got to know Tom, you didn't let this abrupt change of subject upset you. In any case, to try to force some continuity into the conversation was a lost cause.

After a brief search for another dusty tidbit of misinformation, Tom might continue with, "The Kaiser drives the big zeppelin. It's the Hindenburg. The Hindenburg. He drives it you know. The Kaiser!"

As he spoke he would gesture emphatically with his hands while he watched your face very carefully for signs of interest in his words. If you showed an interest, Tom would beam from ear to ear. That in itself was not an altogether desirable thing, however. He was missing the lower half of most of his front teeth.

The only way to dissuade Tom from presenting you with more of his well intended but lopsided facts was to put him on the defensive by asking him questions. One question at a time was enough to slow him down. Two or three quick questions in a row served to discourage further attempts at conversation. With an irritated wave of his hand he would turn and walk off in another direction muttering to himself.

Crazy Tom had a sense of humor, though. One day, in a moment of unrestrained giddiness, he began calling me "Major" and my dog "Kenneth." Thereafter, whenever he did this he dissolved into hysterical laughter.

In recalling that joke of his, I remember that whenever he called me "Major" I would respond as though it were my name. Who, I wonder now, was the REAL village idiot?

Disaster and Tragedy

The 1930s seemed to bring an unusual amount of natural disasters, the most important being the floods of 1936 and 1938 and the hurricane of September 1938. I recall that at the time of the 1936 flood, a

Robert Hames Photo Courtesy Dick Chaisson

Millers River flood waters devastate Athol, Sept. 21, 1938

woman named Annie ran a little Mom and Pop type store down near Batchelor's service station. When the water rose and threatened complete destruction, she and some volunteers saved what they could and then she announced that anyone could help themselves to what was left. Hers must have been a marginally profitable business at best during the Great Depression and she must have lost about everything. I doubt that she had insurance. Her decision, to me, represents the cold, hard, common sense approach to meeting adversity that I associate with New Englanders. It turned out that her store was not destroyed. The basic goodness I admire from my Yankee youth is reflected in the fact that when she reopened the store some weeks after the flood subsided, several people who had helped themselves came by to pay as much as they could for the things they had taken. I contrast that with the impromptu looting under similar circumstances that we see occasionally on our TV screens today. Sometimes I think that maybe the good-ol'-days really were better.

As I recall, there was little warning of the hurricane of 1938 – only a few hours I think. My most vivid memory is of being forced to evacuate our house on Winter Street and moving to my grandmother's house on Wilder Street during the height of the storm. It was

Photo Courtesy Athol Police Department

Captain Earl Grimes

the most destructive tropical storm ever to hit New England. Years later in meteorology school, I got to study about it. It is a part of every course in tropical meteorology.

The only community tragedy that I can recall from my childhood in Athol was the murder of Captain Earl Grimes, an Athol police officer, in 1937. As I recall the incident, a fugitive from New York moved into a "clubhouse" some boys had made close to the railroad tracks below Old Main Street. Their mother called the police when the man refused to leave. That afternoon Captain Grimes and Sergeant Joe McInerny responded. In the process of taking the man in for questioning, he suddenly pulled a sawed-off shotgun and blasted Captain Grimes in the stomach with both barrels. At the sound of the blast, Sergeant McInerny (who was outside the shack at the time) drew his revolver and shot the fugitive as he fumbled for a pistol he had in his hip pocket. The fugitive died from his wounds also.

Captain Grimes was a popular and respected police officer and I recall the whole town being in mourning. There was a general feeling of shock around the area. Things like that just didn't happen in Athol! We had vicariously followed the exploits of such gangsters as Pretty Boy Floyd, Babyface Nelson, John Dillinger, The Barkers, and Bonnie and Clyde elsewhere in the nation. But now gunfire and murder had suddenly come to our peaceful community. The funeral for Captain Grimes was, they said, one of the most heavily attended in the town's history.

To many of us who grew up during the '30s and '40s, the present day lack of respect for the police is appalling. In reality, I suppose the respect we felt was tinged with just a touch of fear. There was something intimidating about the uniform and to "wise off" to a cop was considered pretty foolhardy.

The policeman who made the greatest impression on me during my childhood was Athol's Officer Lashenske. Along with my dad, my boot camp company commander, Douglas MacArthur, and Jack Dempsey, he was one of the five most awesomely authoritative men I've ever seen. His first name was Anthony, I think. His peers call him "Ants." I knew him as "Sir."

I have the impression that peace always reigned in his presence. He strolled his beat or stood on the corner of Main and Exchange streets with the ominous impassivity of a Sherman tank. When he turned his head it was like watching the turret of an M5 searching for a target. When his eyes focused on you it was like looking down the barrel of a 75mm main gun.

He was a quiet man and, I suspect, a gentle man. I doubt that he ever had to raise his voice. I see those Burt Reynolds "good ol' boy" movies nowadays and those TV series featuring undisciplined twits

Photo Dick Chaisson Collection

Officer Anthony Lashenske

making fools of the police and I think, "You wouldn't get away with that crap if you had a cop like Ants Lashenske!"

Coping With The Great Depression

The Great Depression has become so romanticized these days that to have lived through it seems like something to be envied. My generation tends to wear the fact of living through the Great Depression as a badge of honor like having survived the sinking of the Titanic. After so many years, the tragic cost in human lives and misery is pushed to the background or expressed as impersonal statistics. Of course, we in my generation were children and, while we were deprived of many things, it was our parents who bore the hardships and worry. They probably have more difficulty remembering those years with any sense of nostalgia.

My family never missed a meal during even the hardest years, but I'm sure there were many occasions when my parents wondered where the next meal was coming from. It may, at times, have been only pea soup and johnnycake but we never went hungry. And if our fare was something less than seven-course meals during the week, somehow Sunday dinner was usually a sumptuous feast in comparison.

My mother almost always had some sort of roast on Sunday. Her choice depended entirely on which meat was the "best buy" and if there was no "best buy," we killed a chicken. Sunday was also the only day that we had dessert. One of the most vivid impressions that I carry in my memory is of entering our house on cold, snowy, winter Sundays, fingertips and toes aching from near frostbite for having played out too long, and feeling the warmth and savoring the hearty tantalizing aromas of my mother's kitchen. To this day, when my wife prepares a particularly fragrant and tasty meal, I will say, "This reminds me of my mother's Sunday dinners." And by that, I am paying my wife the highest compliment I can think of.

Of course, keeping a family fed is always only part of the problem. Clothing is vital, too, but in the worst years of the Depression, style and fashion took a back seat to practicality. Somewhere, my dad found an outlet for the hardest wearing trousers ever made. They came in only one color — a yucky off-black. I hated them. They were, I think, 40 percent cotton polyester and 60 percent cast iron. They certainly wore like iron. Sir Lancelot should have been so lucky to have a suit made of the stuff.

I remember that if you sat for very long in those trousers when you stood up they retained the shape of your knees. Unless you took them off and stomped on them, you walked around for the rest of the day with little pointed cones protruding from your pant legs. I heard an adult comment one day, "Now that kid has got one helluva case of rickets!" One thing about those trousers, they were heirlooms. You never wore them out — you outgrew them. When that happened I think we stood them in a corner until my younger brothers were big enough to wear them.

It seems there never was a "best" time to wear a hole in your shoe. It was always the "worst possible" time, and a commitment to pay bills always required the postponement of a purchase of shoes. So, we learned to improvise. There used to be cardboard separators in the shredded wheat cereal we so often had for breakfast — for several years they had pictures of children from foreign lands that you could color. My brothers and I discovered that these made great material for covering holes in the soles of your shoes — especially if you coated the material with crayon wax. Except on the wettest days, these repairs would last until you got home from school. And then you were never supposed to take off your "good shoes" anyway.

While I never wore my shoes with holes with the same aplomb that today's generation wears tattered, faded jeans, I never felt any great humiliation. Half the kids in my class had holes in their soles covered with temporary patches at one time or another. The shredded wheat folks missed a chance to make millions by putting shoe outlines in various sizes on their separators instead of pictures to color. The kids of the Great Depression would have appreciated it.

Banks and Money

To my knowledge, my dad never had a bank account until after World War II. During the Depression, he used to say that he "never received a penny but what it wasn't already spoken for." So there was no purpose in having a bank account.

It seems to me that most everyday business was conducted in cash anyway. Even our wages were paid in cash. I can recall that ancient armored car of Starrett's we called "The Black Maria" making its weekly trip each Thursday from the bank to the factories.

I remember being in a bank only once as a child. It was one of those very rare occasions when my dad had a check to cash. The place was like a mausoleum, a Gothic cathedral. There was rich marble everywhere, and polished wood trim and brass fixtures. It was awe-inspiring, and we were the only customers.

There was an eerie quiet about the place, I remember. When my dad put the pen down, the sound echoed. There was a terrible temptation to let out one enormous yell just to hear the echo bounce from wall to wall. But one glance at the portly gentleman seated behind the big desk, behind a glass partition, behind a polished oak railing wiped that flash of inspiration from my mind. He had a glare that would have stopped a cavalry charge.

I followed my dad to a window with a heavy brass plate that said "TELLER." From behind a polished brass grating, peered a face that I instantly mistook for the Wicked Witch of the West. I don't remember a wart on the end of her nose but every other feature conjured up a picture in my mind of bats and bubbling cauldrons. She handled my dad's business quickly and efficiently, as I recall, and I was happy to get out of there. I later learned that all bank tellers are not ugly. In fact, in 1951, I married one.

It surprises me to remember how easy it was to get credit in those days. Not long after I went to work at the UTD in 1942, I went into Louis Fisette's clothing store next to the York Theater to see about buying some clothes "on time." All Louis required to know was my name, that I was Burt Richards' boy, and that I worked for Matt Meany. I walked out of there a half hour later with a top-of-the-line sport coat and a pair of nice trousers. I made a promise to pay a dollar each payday. Mr. Parker, the only employee Louis had, marked the transaction down in a little book — and that was that. I didn't sign anything and no interest was charged. I wish I could get an all wool sport coat like that for fifteen dollars today — or a necktie and a pair of socks, for that matter!

There is a story I recall being told and retold through the years. It seems there was a blind lady who ran a boarding house in Orange. She rented only to men and always insisted that they be hard-working and honest. Asked how she was able to determine that, since she was blind, she said she always demanded to shake the hands of prospective boarders. If their hands were heavily calloused, she figured they must be hard-working. And if they were hard-working they had to be honest.

That story is probably apocryphal but the fact that it was repeated so often suggests that it reflects an attitude about work, self-sufficiency, and character that we admired.

In Praise of Diversity

I have always been a little resentful of the way the movies used to portray New Englanders — especially us small-town and rural folks. It's changing now but you still see examples in the old movies playing on the late-late show. Upper-crust Bostonians were usually shown as spoiled snobs without a lick of common sense, and, I think, non-Bostonians tended to accept that description of the Beacon Hill clique. But rural Yankess were invariably shown as Pa Kettle type hayseeds who had nothing better to do than stand around saying things like "Ayuh," or "Mawnin' comes pretty early around heyuh," or "Gotta get taters hoed and corn all in 'fore snow flies."

Largely on the basis of those old movies, many people from other parts of the country tend to think of New Englanders as a humorless homogeneous mass of melancholy Mayflower descendants. They may concede that there are a few Irish cops and crooked politicians in

Boston and a smattering of Canadian Frenchmen cutting down trees in Maine. But they haven't the foggiest notion of what a diversified mix of nationalities there really is in the picturesque old mill towns and farming communities of New England. My way of convincing people that New England is just as cosmopolitan as any other part of the country is simply to recite the names of some of my school classmates — Krustapentus, Callahan, Piragis, O'Keefe, Plotkin, DePratti, Papageorgas, Robichaud and McGrath, for instance. Now if that isn't an impressive variety of ingredients for the American "melting pot," I don't know what is!

I believe that nowhere else in America could you find a better example of what this nation is all about. So many families that I knew as a boy were relatively new immigrants seeking the American dream. Many of my classmates were first generation native Americans and to my constant envy and wonderment, nearly all of them were bilingual. In some cases, their parents spoke little or no English. I think those of us from old time Yankee families are much the richer for having grown up with the diverse nationalities that make up the population of the Mount Grace region.

While the nationality mix was quite extensive, the only representatives of a racial minority that I can recall living in the area during the 1930s and 1940s were the Chinese who ran the laundry across from the Memorial Hall in Athol. I think only very young children (say, third or fourth graders) found our Chinese citizens to be a curiosity. I can recall at that age following behind the Chinese man chanting:

"Ching Chong Chinaman
Two feet high,
Up came a snowball
And popped him in the eye."

We only did this, of course, when there were several of us to bolster each other's courage. Usually the gentleman ignored us completely. Every now and then, however, he would take action and put us to flight. All he did was stop, turn slowly, and stare at us and we would explode into absolute panic! He didn't threaten us, or gesture at us, or speak to us, or make faces at us. Nothing. He just stared. We would scatter to the four winds and run pell mell until we could run no further. I have no idea why. I suppose it must have been tied to some ludicrous superstition that Caucasian kids generate about Orientals.

When I was a couple of years older I accompanied my dad to the laundry on a few occasions and each time we were treated ever so nicely. My dad was offered a few litchi nuts and I was given a couple of pieces of banana candy. The panic I felt when I was a little kid two years before was replaced by a feeling of sophisticated worldliness as Dad and I shared these goodies from far off China.

Genealogy

I don't remember ever giving much thought to my ancestry as a youngster. I do recall, however, making up a story that I was of Scottish descent and that some vaguely identified relatives had a set of bagpipes and kilts in their attic. It wasn't until my brother Norm, one summer between terms at Boston University, did some research into our forebears that I learned the truth. Lo and behold, Norm discovered that we really are descended from Scots! The first of our ancestors to come to the New World arrived in 1725 and later helped establish the town of Shirley, Mass. Norm did a lot of research into the subject and even visited old graveyards and dug up old town and church records. Years later he traveled to Scotland and, among other things, found the ruins of an old castle or manor house associated with our ancestors. So my childhood imagination was fairly accurate after all. To my knowledge, though, Norman has never discovered any bagpipes or kilts in anybody's attic.

My mother's side of the family, the Websters, have been traced back even further than the Richardses. I have learned this only in recent years from my Aunt Harriette (Webster) Morrell. (Every family ought to have an Aunt Harriette – a witty, walking, talking, encyclopedia of family facts and folklore and diligent caretaker of the family tree.) I think the trail back ends in mid-16th century England. The first of our Websters arrived in New England in 1634 and one of our Websters was, in 1656, a governor of what is now Connecticut. The family moved slowly up through the Connecticut River valley in the ensuing 200 years or so and eventually ended up in the Mount Grace region in the mid-1800s. The old graveyards in the area contain many stones bearing the name Webster.

When I was a very small child, I suppose around four years old, I remember my Great Uncle Virgil ran an antique store in a little old former one-room schoolhouse that stood next to the West Orange Cemetery. It was a fascinating place. It sat well back from the road and, on good days, Great Uncle Virgil would display some of his larger items in the yard. These usually included two or three of those ancient bicycles with the enormous front wheel and little tiny rear wheel. From a child's perspective, the front wheels looked 10 feet high. Those bikes surely must have been for adults only. I think a kid would get a nosebleed just climbing up to the seat.

The school is gone now and the cemetery has spread further west over the years, occupying the site of the old school. My Grandmother and Grandfather Webster first met at that one-room schoolhouse as child classmates in the 1880s. They are buried together in the litttle cemetery only a few feet from the spot where they met.

Chapter 4

The House On Wilder Street

On Grandparents

Now that I'm a grandparent, I've tried to rationalize the difference in the attitudes of grandchildren to grandparents and vice versa. I have come to the conclusion that there is little special about the relationship from a grandparent's point of view. I think we tend to love our grandchildren in very much the same way as we loved our children at that age. If you're lucky there are, of course, some nice benefits to being a GRANDparent – no diaper changing, no formulas to prepare, and no 2 o'clock feedings, for example. And, when their parents aren't looking, you can spoil 'em rotten!

But, in remembering my childhood, grandparents are really something quite special to a child and are viewed very differently than parents. Grandparents are, in my memory, more tolerant and less disciplinary than parents, more appreciative of a child's littlest accomplishments, always ready with praise, and much more susceptible to childish pleadings. They are sometimes even allies against peremptory parental decisions.

I had plenty of parents to go around. My folks separated in 1933 and each remarried. I went to live with my dad and stepmother in 1936. I was less fortunate with grandparents, however, having (in effect) only one of each as compared with the two complete sets of grandparents my friends usually had.

My Grandmother Webster died when I was quite young and so I barely knew her. My memory of her is very limited – a stern-faced but loving, doting grandmother who made the best crullers and sugared doughnut holes in the world.

I only met my Grandfather (Fred) Richards once. In the summer of 1941 a few of us visited him in Sherbrooke, Quebec, where he spent the last fifteen years or so of his life. He was a giant of a man with the massive shoulders of a former blacksmith and a large heavy face. But he was pretty much confined to a wheelchair, having had a leg amputated a couple years before. I had heard stories all my life of his physical prowess – family folklore having it that he was widely acclaimed as the strongest man ever to live in Winchendon. I sometimes wish I could have met him in his youth rather than his old age if for no other reason than to sustain that larger-than-life, admiring verbal portrait drawn by his sons, Burt and Charlie. As it was we never got to know each other at all in my short visit. He seemed not to take a whole lot of interest in me and I felt very awkward in his presence. I wrote to him a few times during World War II and sent him some small gifts from Shanghai when the war was over but he never acknowledged them. He died in 1946 and I went to his funeral. I remember being terribly embarrassed at my inability to mourn at his graveside while my father, uncle and aunts poured out their grief in great spasms of genuine emotion. And so it is that, for all intents and purposes, I never had a Grandfather Richards. He was more a distant legend, a storybook hero who lived only in the words of others. But I will continue to pass along the family stories of his strength, honesty and courage. I owe that to my dad who knew and loved him well.

My Grandfather (Albert) Webster was very much what I guess could be called a typical grandfather. He was white-haired (actually his hair turned white when he was in his early 20's, I'm told), a little on the portly side, good natured, generous to a fault (with his grandchildren at least), and as loving and doting as his wife had been. Since he lived in Orange and, after 1935, we grandkids lived elsewhere, I didn't see Grandpa Webster too often but each time was a memorable experience. Each summer for a few years he would take his grandchildren on a special outing — often to Benson's Animal Farm in Hudson, N.H. Along the way, I remember, there was a straight stretch of road in a remote area where Grandpa would crank his little '36 Dodge coupe up to 60 miles-per-hour for a second or two until we all had a chance to read the speedometer. "Wow," we would say to one another, "a mile a minute!" If I had heard about the speed of sound at that time I would probably have guessed that we were pretty darn close to it.

There were some memorable Christmases at Grandpa's apartment in the Plotkin Block in Orange during the last few years of his life. The vision of him and those holidays that I carry in my mind is one of a thoroughly happy man surrounded by a loving family, and glowing with contentment and pleasure.

I cannot recall him ever being angry. That's obviously a false impression, but it's one my brother Norm shares, too. My dad, however, used to tell of an instance when I was very young when Grandpa Webster probably had homicidal impulses concerning me — at that time his only grandchild. That was when with a rake handle I knocked every pane of glass out of his garage on Hamilton Avenue and followed it up by trying to paint his new black Hudson yellow. I do not remember that incident and, for the sake of my memory of my grandfather, it's probably just as well!

My Grandmother Richards holds a very special and precious place in my memory. My brothers, sisters and cousins would most likely agree that she was the perfect grandma. Of all my grandparents, I knew her best. She was a very important part of my life.

Eugenia "Jenny" Richards, whose maiden name was LaRoux, was of French-Canadian descent and grew up around Leominster somewhere. For many years she was a farmer's wife in New Boston before Fred gave up farming in 1916 and moved to Green Street in Athol. A short time later, during World War I, Fred was offered a good paying position in Detroit, Michigan. While her husband went on ahead, Jenny packed up their belongings and the children and followed. After a couple years, Jenny, who did not like city life, wanted to return to Massachusetts. Sight unseen, her husband bought the house at 84 Wilder Street in Athol and Jenny brought the family back home. Fred Richards never returned to his family. He stayed on in Michigan until sometime in the early thirties when he moved to Canada.

The house at 84 Wilder Street is an anchor in my memory. All during the Depression years when my family moved so frequently, Grandma's house remained constant and unchanging, certain and sure like a wooden Rock of Gibraltar. No matter where we were liv-

The house on Wilder Street (about 1940)

ing we visited Grandma often. For all my childhood years it was a house filled with love, laughter, compassion, joy, warmth and comfort — a family homestead in the most complete meaning of that term.

Grandma Richards was rather short, somewhat plump, white haired, and a strict but ever so gentle disciplinarian. However, I have seen her on occasion, reduce my hard-as-nails father to a blushing, apologetic schoolboy simply by raising an eyebrow and saying, "Now, Burton!" Usually that happened when Dad accidentally spoke a bad word in her presence. Grandma brooked absolutely no bad language in her house. One time, under questioning about what I was studying in school, I blurted, "The Grand Coulee Darn!"

I have heard that she had quite a hot temper but I only saw it once. When I was about ten, I went racing into her kitchen one day without knocking and slammed the door behind me with a resounding crash. It must have been one of her bad days because she lit into me with all guns blazing. I was absolutely flabbergasted. The sweetest, dearest, most gentle woman in all the world was suddenly transformed into a raging lady ogre about to skin me alive. She didn't strike me but, coming from her, the scolding she gave me hurt much worse. I was humiliated and virtually reduced to tears.

We lived next door at the time, in the Carey house at the end of the street. I went straight home and told my mother that I wasn't ever going to Grandma's house again — at least for a skillion, jillion years. My resolve lasted all of three days, I guess, and then I got word from my brothers that Grandma had made an applesauce cake and was saving me a piece. She greeted me with the same old love and affection that I was accustomed to. I'm pretty sure that my piece of applesauce cake that day was quite a lot bigger than my brothers got.

The Secret Knock

Whenever we went to visit my grandmother, my dad would knock "dum dum de dum dum, dum dum." My grandmother recognized the knock and would call "come in" without having to get up to answer the door. As a child I always considered that knock to be the "famous old Richards secret knock." (I never tried to reconcile fame with secrecy.)

One day I was at a friend's house when a neighbor dropped by and, to my consternation, used the famous old Richards secret knock! I was shocked and dismayed. Someone had compromised what I con-

"Jenny Richards — the perfect Grandma"

sidered to be a sacred family trust.

Henceforth, I worried, my grandmother would not be safe in her own home. Any stranger might knock "dum dum de dum dum, dum dum" and she would call "come in." I visualized a terrible scene in which a sneering, leering, dirty-no-good intruder would tie Grandma in her Morris chair. Then he'd open the top drawer in Grandma's hutch which no one was EVER allowed to enter. (I always suspected that there were riches and valuables stored in that drawer.) And then the evil intruder would find what he was really looking for behind the lower doors in Grandma's corner cupboard. Here my cousins and I were allowed free access. Here was kept such things as the Monopoly game, the wind-up British tank, the Game of India, a musical spinning top, a doll or two, the checkerboard, and a half-dozen or so toy soldiers — all irreplaceable items of infinite value. And, of course, all the fabulous family heirlooms would fall into the hands of the intruder — the portrait of General John "Black Jack" Pershing, Uncle Charlie's drumsticks, the wind-up Victorola, the little glass ball with a winter scene that snowed when you shook it. All these things would be lost forever because someone slipped and let out the secret of the famous Richards knock — or (more painful to contemplate), purposely gave it away!

Who would have done such a thing? It must have been an "inside job," I reasoned. But who in our family would betray such a trust? I finally decided it must have been my little brother Mac.

The Lance

I had never trusted Mac from that darkest of days in my childhood when he broke my marvelous lance "Excalibur." My lance was one of those absolutely perfect things a boy finds but once in his life. It was just about the right length (around six feet long, I guess) and just the right circumference and weight and of exquisitely grained wood. It was tapered at one end and I sometimes attached a red rag to the tip as a banner or guidon. It could also be used as a spear. Oh, the pulse-quickening, blood-tingling charges I led with that lance! And, oh, the tremendous odds I and my imaginary stalwart band of loyal cohorts overcame! Sometimes I was Robin Hood beating the daylights out of the Sheriff of Nottingham; sometimes I was Montezuma or Crazy Horse beating the daylights out of encroaching white men; sometimes I was Tarzan beating the daylights out of some bad guys trying to find the lost graveyard of the elephants. And, sometimes I was a captain in the 21st Lancers beating the daylights out of the Whirling Dervishes at Omdurman. I think I can safely claim that I never lost a battle with that lance.

Then one day while I was at school my little brother Mac got hold of it. He went into the 4-ft. by 6-ft. "clubhouse" that Clinton Fitch and I had built in my back yard and took Excalibur down from its place on the Golden Wall of Honor (we had painted one wall yellow). After that, who knows how that glorious weapon was misused and defiled! When I arrived home from school it was lying in two pieces in the yard. Mac was only about four years old at the time but he would never have lived to see five if I had had my way! My search for a suitable substitute lance was in vain. How can you match absolute perfection?

My brother Mac is now a reputable upstanding, and successful businessman in Olympia, Washington. But I'll tell you this – even to this day I will never leave another lance around where he can get his hands on it! I've since decided, though, that he probably was innocent of compromising our famous old Richards secret knock.

Holidays

The house at 84 Wilder Street was the focal point of all our full-family holiday celebrations. On the Fourth of July we would gather along with my uncles, aunts, and cousins at Grandma's house to share our fireworks. None of us could afford a great number of fireworks but by pooling them in Grandma's back yard we always had a spectacular Fourth.

At the depth of the Great Depression, we usually gathered at Grandma's house to celebrate Christmas. Mostly it was the children who received gifts. There just wasn't enough money for the adults to exchange presents. We gathered in Grandma's front room to open our gifts and to entertain one another. Each child was expected to perform and I was usually made to sing "Home on the Range." I say "made" because I was a reluctant performer. I have always loved to sing and, in later years, sang on Armed Forces Radio, and in a couple of amateur stage shows and nightclubs – but never as a soloist. I was always by temperament and talent better suited to singing with a group. I could carry a tune fairly well and always sang the lead in trios and quartets while better voices sang the harmony parts. So, on those Christmas nights at Grandma's I would balk at having to stand alone in the middle of her parlor and do my thing. I would mumble hastily and self-consciously through "Home on the Range" at twice the tempo at which it was supposed to be sung. Occasionally, my dad would "coax" me to try again suggesting such songs as "My Bonnie Lies Over the Ocean" or "Camptown Races." Neither of these added much to the Christmas spirit, of course, but at least they were easy songs to sing and satisfied the family rule that all the kids participate in the festivities. I think my cousins David and Eleanor shared my attitude about performing, but two other cousins, Lorraine and Marilyn Kingsbury, were terrific singers who went on to sing professionally. I was always happy to have them sing first because they invariably got requests for encores which at least postponed my much dreaded moment in the spotlight.

Once the children's solo performances were out of the way, we all joined in singing lots of old favorites as well as the traditional Christmas songs – always saving "Silent Night" for last. My dad and Aunt Linda played the piano. Well, really, it was Aunt Linda who played – Dad just hit a key every now and then to justify his sitting on the piano bench. Uncle Charlie had once been a drummer and, though he had long since sold his drum, he still had his drumsticks. He provided the beat using Grandma's checkerboard as a drum. Wilder Street really rocked on those Christmas Eves when the Richards clan gathered.

Of course everyone came to visit Grandma on Mother's Day wearing carnations and all dressed up in our Sunday best. She always expressed total surprise at the gifts and cards we brought her and told us repeatedly that we "shouldn't have."

Halloweens during the Depression were also shared at Grandma's house. I don't remember any elaborate costumes but Grandma always had an appropriate response – cringing in feigned horror before a 3-ft. high, 4-year-old in a five-cent werewolf mask, for example. We bobbed for apples in her washtub and strained on tip-toe to reach (with our teeth – no hands) doughnuts hung on strings above our heads. There were other games, too, and at some point in the evening we would all line up in the kitchen with our jack-o-lanterns and Grandma would turn out the lights. Just as we were busy admiring each other's jack-o-lanterns in the darkness, my dad or Uncle Pete would burst into the kitchen from the cellar or hall in a hideous

Dracula get-up and holding a flashlight under his chin to make the face even more grotesque. At the same time, Aunt Linda would let out a piercing shriek that made your blood run cold. Grandma was ready with the lights to restore order but there was panic and pandemonium for a few seconds, let me tell you! It was only Grandma who could console the littlest ones when it was all over. And while she was doing that, my mother and Aunt Evelyn would take the neapolitan brick ice cream from the ice box for serving. As we left, everyone including Grandma expressed a certainty that we would have nightmares that night.

During "shop" in the seventh or eighth grade, about 1939 or 1940, at Riverbend School, I made Grandma a lamp shaped like a cat holding an umbrella. I suppose almost every grandmother in Athol got one sooner or later. When I went off to war in 1944, she said she'd keep it burning for me until I returned. I have no idea if she meant that literally. In any case, that little lamp kept working for a few more years at least.

I rejoined the Navy in March of 1948 and never saw Grandma Richards again. She died that summer. I was in Kodiak, Alaska – too distant to attend her funeral, but I have visited her grave at the Highland Cemetery in Athol. The memory of her – her strength, her constancy, and her love – will be with me all the days of my life. As will my memory of the house on Wilder Street.

A Christmas Past

I think everyone has a fond memory or two about family holidays. Nearly 30 years ago my dad wrote me a letter filled with nostalgic reminiscences of a boyhood Christmas on the family farm in New Boston. It tells of a different house and a younger "Jenny" but the same warmth and family affection I remember from the house on Wilder Street are there. The little community of New Boston near Waterville was wiped out by the Birch Hill dam project much as Prescott, Dana, and other towns were obliterated by the Quabbin project. Apart from the seasonal aspect of the letter, it provides some insights into what life was like in rural New England "not long after the turn of the century." The letter, dated December 16, 1956, reads as follows:

"Dear Ken and Family,

"Nothing on television tonite, so as I sit here smoking my pipe, I've been comparing this Christmas season with one nearly half a century ago. These evenings of nostalgia become more frequent as one grows older. Tonite my mind goes back to a Christmas season not long after the turn of the century. Back to an old New England farm. So cold that the snow has a crust that will bear the weight of a horse and sleigh. The frost so penetrating, that as you breathe, it threatens to close your nostrils. An awe-inspiring silence in the night, so great that the sound of a man's footsteps on the frozen snow carry a quarter of a mile.

"I can see my father coming in from his chores, his felt boots thumping and hear him say, 'It's nigh onto thirty below zero right now, it will hit forty by morning.' He sits down in his big chair by the stove, adjusts his glasses, turns the kerosene lamp up a bit, and picks up last Sunday's paper. But the contrast from the outside cold to the warmth of the room is too much. In less than two minutes, the sound of gentle snores issues from his chair.

"In a farming community of that era, there was very little diversification. The mid-week prayer meeting was an event not to be overlooked. An occasional box social, and a monthly kitchen dance constituted practically all the amusement obtainable. Therefore, in this week, the week before Christmas, there was an undercurrent of excitement throughout the community. Not only was there the church supper, but an entertainment.

"The party lines were busy with preparatory discussions, and I can see my mother now, as she stood by the wall phone, a look of quiet enjoyment on her face, as she agreed to bring two chocolate cakes.

"Finally, the long awaited night arrived, mother bustling around, getting us freshly-scrubbed youngsters into our 'Sunday clothes,' father stoking the stoves with rock maple chunks, my brother swinging up to the front door with the 'two seater' sleigh, the horses impatiently stamping anxious to be off. After the lap robes were carefully tucked in, we were off, sleigh bells tinkling, great waves of steam arising from the horses' breaths.

"The eager anticipation with which we looked forward can only happen to a small child. Oh, the wonder of it all. The supper, the entertainment, composed strictly of local talent, the Christmas tree, each child receiving a little sack of hard candy, an item that children were not as familiar with as today's generation.

"And then, the crowning achievement of the evening. One of the more prosperous farmers of the locality produced a square box with a huge horn attached to it. After much ado and fussing, this box emitted music!! The gasps of amazement from adult as well as child!! A real gramophone!! What in the world will they invent next, etc., etc. I'm sure we all went home feeling quite sophisticated.

"The next day was Christmas, and we children had all hung our stockings, of course. The first one to awaken immediately aroused the others for the frantic dash downstairs. We found that Santa had treated us all exactly alike. In our stockings were an orange, a banana, some nuts, and some hard candy. All of these items were only seen at Christmas any year, so in reality, it was a wonderful treat, and appreciated fully as much as the expensive gifts that have to be given today.

"I can well recollect that Christmas afternoon, we all gathered in the 'front room' and my oldest sister, who had contrived to learn to play the organ, accompanied us, while we sang 'Silent Night,' and 'Away in the Manger.' Thus ended as happy a Christmas as I have ever known. To us, it wasn't a small Christmas, it was beautiful!

"People are more or less apt to feel that one should forget the past and live with the present, but I think it is rather nice to relive events that were happy milestones that we pass in the short span of years allotted us.

"Goodnight,
"Love, Dad"

Chapter 5

'Don't You Know There's A War On?'

I suppose anyone over the age of 50 can recall exactly where they were when they first received news of the attack on Pearl Harbor. I remember that on that fateful Sunday, Dec. 7, 1941, I was at Cliff Upham's house in Petersham when one of his sisters came outside to tell us the news. I don't remember our immediate reaction but after I got home and talked with my dad I began to understand the implications of the attack. My dad hoped that the war would be over quickly but doubted it. I would probably be in it, he told me, and like most teenagers, I was rarin' to go even though I had only just turned 15. The next day, all the students at Petersham Center School were assembled to hear a radio broadcast of President Roosevelt's "day of infamy" speech asking the Congress to declare war. Mr. Arnold then led the student body in a brief prayer for the safety of the nation and the men who would do the fighting.

Athol had already suffered its first casualty several weeks before Pearl Harbor. Harold Britt, who lived up on Wilder Street near my grandmother, had lost his life when the USS Reuben James, an old "4-pipe" destroyer, was sunk by a German U-boat in the North Atlantic. I can't recall if any local boys were among the casualties at Pearl Harbor. Before the war ended, there would be all too many gold stars hanging in the windows of homes in the towns north of Quabbin. And all too many young men would return crippled and maimed.

In my box of souvenirs, I have the blue star banner that hung in my mother's window during my service in World War II. It's faded and cracked and the tassles are tangled and frayed. I should have thrown it out years ago I suppose — it never meant much to me. But I know how much those banners meant to the families back home. A blue star was for a family member in the armed services; a gold star represented a family member who had died in the service. They were displayed with great pride during the last period in our history when military service was considered, by the vast majority of Americans of all ages, to be a prideful thing.

The War Effort

It took several months for America to fully gear up for the war effort. Food and gas rationing came in the spring of 1942, as I recall. I still have my ration book with many stamps unused. There were warnings against hoarding, which must have seemed ridiculous to a nation just then beginning to climb out of the depths of the Great Depression. Most folks I knew around Athol had barely enough money to buy this week's food and fuel, much less lay in a hoard for the duration of the war. Americans were also encouraged to start "victory gardens" but most everyone I knew already had small vegetable gardens — a hold-over from the same Great Depression. There were scrap drives and in one way or another we all did our part for the war effort. For those whose patriotism seemed to wane, there was the ultimate put-down — "Don't you know there's a war on?" There were occasional victory bond drives and I seem to remember that Dinah Shore and a troupe of entertainers made a pitch from the steps of Memorial Hall one day.

The best example I recall of a citizen's support for the men in uniform was Della Bemis and her "super-duper" ice cream sundae. Every local serviceman returning on leave was given a free "soopuh-doopuh" when stopping in at Bemis' store on the uptown common. Della, as sweet and caring a woman as ever lived, ran the soda fountain in the store. Her duper-duper was to ice cream what the Eiffel Tower is to architecture. It was served, as I recall, in a dish that was about the size of a No. 3 washtub. The base of the super-duper was four or five scoops of different flavors of ice cream, a sliced banana, a shot of each type of syrup that Della served, marshmallow, all smothered under a mountain of whipped cream, sprinkled with nuts and jimmies, and topped with three or four maraschino cherries. The super-duper was not, as I recall, on the menu. It had no price. In fact, it was priceless. It was a special treat reserved for servicemen. The Della Bemis Super-Duper should be listed in the Guinness Book of Records. I wonder if Della ever received any official recognition for her patriotism. Anyone who ever stuffed themselves on a super-duper would agree she should have been given the keys to the city.

Civil defense was a big thing in every town and we all had blackouts. Voluteer air raid wardens made their appointed rounds to check that every household complied with the regulations. Mr. "Skiff" Anderson was our warden in Petersham, I remember. Every household received literature about what to do in case of an air raid and each school had air raid drills periodically. As I recall, we all took the drills quite seriously. I think we imagined Hitler telling Goering, "I want you to bomb Boston, New York, and Washington, D. C. — but first thing you must obliterate Petersham!" Or maybe we thought if Petersham was not a likely target, then perhaps carelessness on our part would make it a beacon by which a German bomber could navigate. We imagined, I think, a Luftwaffe pilot saying to his navigator, "Look! That light down there is from Burt Richards' kitchen. New York must be that way."

Of course no enemy planes ever reached America but almost before the smoke had cleared at Pearl Harbor we were bombarded with hastily written war songs. Most, like "We'll Knock the Hit Out of Hitler" and "When Those Little Yellow Bellies Meet the Cohens and the Kellys" and "We'll Knock the Japs Right Into the Laps of the Nazis" were destined for quick and merciful oblivion. I recall Mr. Henry Wheeler, the itinerant music teacher for the area schools, lamenting the fact that no songs of the caliber of "Over There" and "Grand Old Flag" (from World War I) were being written.

Signing Up

I wanted to join a military service on the day I turned 17 but my dad managed to deter me for a few months. Finally, in the spring of 1944, Albine Piragis and I got our parents' permission and went off to Boston to join the Navy. We had hoped to go in together, like several other Athol guys, and perhaps be assigned to the same ship. Bureaucratic red tape intervened, though, and he was called to duty a few weeks before me.

The period between acceptance and actual departure for military service was a busy and exciting time. There was no place for thoughts or apprehensions about separation from loved ones, or of the hardships that lay ahead, or even of becoming a casualty. If any arose, they were quickly swept away by the incessant patriotic propaganda on the radio, in the movies, and in newspapers and magazines. In the patriotic climate of wartime America, a commitment to military service was regarded, by most, with approval and admiration. For a young single man, the new found attention of young women, the well-intentioned advice and admonitions of the older generation, and the proud doting of family and friends served to fill one's mind and blot out the realities of what lay ahead. I think our minds skipped right over the intervening months or years from that night when we would kiss our girlfriends goodbye to the day when we would return with a chest full of ribbons to the outstretched arms of a sweetheart who hadn't sat under the apple tree with anyone else.

During the last hectic week or so at home, we were besieged by well-wishers. It was a period "in the spotlight" never to be forgotten. I remember being asked (usually by men too old for military service) to "kill a few of those Nips (or Germans) for me." I always agreed, of course, and by the time I finally left, I imagine that at least a battalion of Japanese were condemned to death at my hands. Others (usually older ladies) asked that I keep my eye out for their nephews or cousins or sons who were out there "somewhere" in one war theater or other. "If you ever run into Jimmy, be sure to tell him Auntie Beth says hello," they would say. I must have left home with a list of 20 of 30 names of people I barely knew or had never heard of before to whom I was supposed to say "Hi." I'm sure every departing serviceman had a similar list and we all gave our solemn promises to such requests. I know that if on the unlikely chance I had run into Jimmy, I surely would have said "Hi" from Auntie Beth. On the other hand, despite my brave promises, if I had ever run into a live, armed Japanese, I probably would have fainted dead away!

On my last day of work in the shipping room at UTD, Mrs. Newell brought in a cake and I was presented with a card and an envelope containing some money. And, one evening, I and a couple of others were given a farewell party at the Unitarian Church in Petersham. It was a tradition at those functions that the departing enlistee was given a pocket New Testament, a pair of black or khaki socks (depending on which service the person was entering), and a khaki colored moneybelt.

It goes without saying that the New Testament and the socks were well and truly appreciated and used. But I have often wondered just how many servicemen ever really used a moneybelt. The things didn't come with any instructions. There were cords and strings and flaps and snaps — all very complicated. I tried mine on once. We were given a six-hour liberty at boot camp and after showering in preparation for the big event I decided that the first thing to put on was my moneybelt. After fiddling with it for a while, I eventually got it to stay around my waist. In the mirror, though, it looked like some weird article of intimate apparel designed by Frederick of Hollywood — a cross between a saddle bag and a garter belt. I never put mine on again.

A day or so before I left I got a letter from Albine, who was well into boot camp at Sampson, N.Y. In the most emphatic terms he advised me not to join. Too late! On the morning of June 1, 1944, my mother drove me to the Athol depot to catch the train for Springfield (my dad had said his goodbyes before leaving for work). When the train pulled in, all the machismo and bravado that had swelled up over the past few weeks suddenly evaporated. I kissed my mother goodbye and climbed aboard the train, afraid to look back for fear of showing the doubts and second thoughts that were racing through my mind. In Greenfield, where I had to change trains, I met another young man headed for Springfield and the Navy. He was from a small town in Vermont and the chances are that he was as scared and apprehensive as I was. But we told each other the exaggerated personal tales of debauchery, seduction, intemperance, and derring-do that young men like to share and so put our unadmitted fears temporarily out of mind. The next day I passed the physical examination, was sworn in, and left immediately for the horrors and inhumanities that, according Albine, awaited me at the Naval Training Center, Sampson.

Boot Leave

I finished boot camp on the 3rd of August and was at sea on the 17th. So much for stateside duty! In the interim, though, I had a seven-day leave. It was to be the only leave I would have during my first tour of duty in the Navy. I knew that some Athol men who went in the service early in the war weren't given any boot leave and instead went directly to their first assignment. So I was thankful for those seven days.

For those of us fortunate enough to get a leave, the days at home were much too short and far too fleeting. It was wonderful to be with your family again but there was the mandatory visit to all the relatives to show off your uniform. For most of us, this probably ranked well down on the list of most exciting things to do while on boot leave. Dating girls and visiting friends of your own age group were much more appealing. A visit to my former co-workers at the UTD shipping room was one of my first stops. I was greeted more as though I had just come from taking Guadalcanal single-handedly than returning from boot camp. Jim Cosgrove, Charlie Robinson, Mrs. Newell, Stan Paluilis, Winnie Rawson, Mr. Meany and the rest made my visit truly memorable. I went away feeling only slightly behind Eisenhower, MacArthur, and Nimitz in relative importance to the war effort.

The only memento I have of that brief interlude is a snapshot with Cliff Upham who was home on leave from the Army Air Force. There certainly were lots of area servicemen home on leave. You could hardly drive down Main Street anytime without seeing a uniform or two. My leave was over all too quickly.

Returning to duty was not quite as difficult as it had been to go away for the first time. The Navy was no longer the frightening unknown it had been a couple months before. And, too, there was always the optimistic hope that you too would get another leave soon — maybe for the Christmas holidays! It didn't happen for me but I'm sure some area servicemen were luckier.

Christmas 1944

I remember my first Christmas away from home — 1944. My ship was at anchor in Humboldt Bay, New Guinea. The skipper had okayed the piping of Christmas music over the PA system and late that evening I went back to the fantail to be alone. One of the last songs they played before "Taps" was Bing Crosby's "White Christmas." The words brought back memories of Athol during the holiday season with crowds of people along Main Street stomping through the snow to shop at Fishman's, W.T Grant's, and Woolworth's. I could envision, too, Petersham lying under a blanket of snow like a real life rendering by Currier and Ives. And there I was on that damn ship, staring at that stinking damn island, in that god-forsaken part of the world. I don't think I've ever been so lonely in my life. Bing's song didn't help things a bit. I admit it, I cried. Looking back at it from a broader perspective, though, I didn't really have it half bad. Men were dying that Christmas Day in a place called "the Bulge" in Belgium and in other spots around the world. No, I was lucky to be where I was I guess. But you couldn't convince me of that at the time. Now, every time I hear "White Christmas" I think of that Christmas evening — and of the old home town.

War Experiences

I have always likened my experiences in World War II to arriving at the scene of an auto or train accident after the ambulances have left. In the course of my travels I came upon the wrecks of airplanes, hulks of ships, blasted fortifications, and crumbled ruins of cities and towns. But the battles had already moved on. Only the stunned witnesses and innocent victims of what happened there remained. I never shot at anyone and no one ever shot at me, but on several occasions I watched from a distance while other people fought.

I particularly remember one Sunday afternoon while at anchor in Manila Bay in March or April of 1945. I was sitting on the forecastle with a few shipmates eating an ice cream sundae when someone pointed to a large flight of B-24's approaching in a neat, precise formation. As we watched, the planes crossed over the bay and then turned majestically north over the hills beyond Manila. Suddenly the earth beneath them erupted in hundreds of blips of fire and great billows of dark smoke and dust. It was only then that we Sunday afternoon loiterers realized that we were watching a real, honest-to-God bombing mission!

Someone said, "This is absurd!"

And it was. Here we sailors were basking in the peaceful, drowsy, tropical heat of a Philippines afternoon, enjoying ice cream and soft drinks, engaging in banter and horseplay and, within our sight, a real life-and-death drama was being enacted over the Japanese lines in the hills beyond the city. The planes completed their bombing run, wheeled over the bay once again and, still in precise formation, disappeared into the clouds over the Bataan Peninsula. The incongruity of that Sunday afternoon has never left me.

On November 10, 1944, I was on the island of Manus in the Admiralties in the South Pacific awaiting transportation to New Guinea. That morning I was assigned to a work detail, transporting and unloading truckloads of stores and supplies.

We had not yet completed unloading our first truck when the island was suddenly rocked by an earth-shaking explosion. The ground trembled and the big Quonset hut warehouse we were in shook as though in a typhoon. There had been an air raid warning the day before (a false alarm, I think) and of course that was our first thought. Someone in charge ordered us to go to a ditch or trench outside. There were no further explosions, however, and no sirens or gunfire so we went back and finished unloading the truck.

On our return to the dock area, we rounded a hill and Seeadler Harbor came into view. We noticed a lot of frantic activity and a pall of now thinning black smoke lying over the water but no one seemed to know what had happened. Rumors flew throughout the day and it wasn't until sometime that evening that we learned an ammunition ship, the USS Mount Hood, had blown up. There were only a half dozen or so survivors and they had been on the island at the time of the explosion. Everyone aboard, some 350 officers and crewmen, had perished instantly. Nearly 100 others were killed and scores wounded on nearby ships and small craft. A board of inquiry, later, was unable to find what caused the explosion.

After the war, a bunch of us were sitting in the Puritan Restaurant on Main Street drinking coffee and telling sea stories when I mentioned that tragic event. It was then that I learned for the first time (I don't know who told me) that Bobby Adams had been on that ship and was killed in the explosion. Bobby used to live up around Vine Street as I recall. His brother Sam and I were classmates at the Highland School and later at Riverbend.

With the knowledge that an acquaintance from Athol had died at that instant, the terrible roar of that explosion found renewed clarity in my memory. I remember it vividly even today.

I think of how two teenage kids from a small New England town arrived at that moment in time within a couple of miles of one another at a remote Pacific island. One died at a little after 8 o'clock that morning. The other lived to middle age to write a word or two about the event — and to wonder all his days about the mysterious workings of fate and destiny.

New England Accent

Like most Yankees out of their element, I took an awful lot of ribbing in the Navy about my New England accent. I learned very quickly, however, that there was money to be made with my pronunciation. Most pre-World War II dictionaries showed a preference for the Yankee pronunciation of words like laugh, calf, aunt, and half over "laff," "caff," "ant," and "haff." It was easy to lure many a hardheaded Texan or Brooklynite into a trap. "Betcha a buck!" I'd say and off we'd go to the ships's library where the big, unabridged Webster's dictionary was kept. I must have made 10 or 15 dollars over the course of 18 months on that ship. Several years later during the Korean War my little game backfired. My new ship had a post-war dictionary and those damn Texans and Brooklynites had had their way — their pronunciation is now preferred!

It's really amazing to me that umpteen miles from home in some god-forsaken part of the world you can run into the guy from next door. I remember one day in the summer of 1945, in the Philippines, I woke up to find Woody Anderson's ship, the USS Gillette, in the squadron of destroyer escorts that had arrived during the night. Woody had lived just around the corner from me in Petersham. I had received a letter from him only a few weeks before and it still had an Atlantic fleet address. With the end of the war in Europe, however, his was one of many ships transferred to the Pacific. I visited him on his ship (and was promptly put to work in an "all hands" working party) and then he returned with me to my ship. When he left I gave him a couple of gallons of ice cream – an almost non-existent luxury in a destroyer escort. We planned to meet again in Manila for a real liberty but instead his ship went up north for the final battles against Japan. It wasn't until about a year later that we saw one another again – in Petersham.

Songs of World War II

It has occurred to me that the story of World War II could almost be told with the songs from that era. Despite the fact that some of the songs were of the somewhat foolish smash-the-enemy type, there were beautiful and memorable compositions.

I suppose our songs have always reflected our times and our moods, but it was especially true in those war years. Even before we entered the war our songs empathized with the people of Europe as nation after nation fell beneath the hobnailed boots of the conquering Germans. "The Last Time I Saw Paris" is a classic of the early days of World War II. "My Sister and I" is another example. It told the tale of Dutch refugees driven from their homeland. "White Cliffs of Dover" promised that peace would come again and that bluebirds would indeed return one day to replace the war planes over the English Channel coast.

Then came Pearl Harbor and songs like "We Did It Before And We Can Do It Again" and "This Is Worth Fighting For" which expressed our confidence and resolve. As a change of pace we enjoyed insulting Adolph Hitler with "Der Fuehrer's Face" – a song which included, as I recall, a "Bronx cheer" in appropriate places.

As America geared for war and the armed services began to swell with new recruits, "This Is The Army, Mr. Jones" described the problems of changing from civilian to military life. "GI Jive" was a "hep" version of the same theme. The songs made the transition seem a lot easier than it really was. And then there was the Andrews Sisters' big hit, "Boogie Woogie Bugle Boy of Company B." It told of a jivey army that "jumped" to a groovy bugler at reveille. I never met a soldier who was in that army!

I remember a song called "Johnny Doughboy Found A Rose In Ireland." The title sounds like it came from World War I, but it was popular in the early '40s. I'm not sure when "Johnny Doughboy" became "GI Joe" but it must have been fairly early in the war. While the British "Tommies" have always fought the German "Jerries," we called the Germans "Huns" in the First World War and "Krauts" in the Second. What with the "Eyeties," "Frenchies," "Limeys," "Japs," "Nips," "Aussies," "Swabbies," "Jarheads," "Dogies," "Hooligans," "Fly Guys," and a hundred other names it was hard to tell the combatants without a program.

There were a few songs, I remember, that were about military action. Those that come to mind are "Praise The Lord And Pass The Ammunition," "A Guy 24 In A B-29," "Johnny Got A Zero," and "Comin' In On A Wing And A Prayer." There probably were others but none were what you'd call "big hits."

Servicemen wanted songs of love not war. And it was the love songs that were most popular. The song title "A Boy In Khaki, A Girl In Lace" expresses the recurrent theme. (It wasn't until late in the war, I think, that songwriters finally stopped calling us "soldier boy" or "sailor boy"!) Many of the love songs were terribly mushy and sickeningly sentimental — at least they seem so today. It's a bit uncomfortable to remember myself being deeply affected by all that sentimentality — getting all cow-eyed, weak-kneed, and weepy over those saccharin love song lyrics. But then there is another side of me that remembers that remarkable naivete and innocence with a sense of yearning and nostalgia. There comes a subliminal desire in middle age to relive those coming-of-age years — to have another opportunity to lose one's innocence.

A few songs like, "I'm In Love With The Girl I Left Behind Me" seemed to express GI Joe's promise of fidelity. In some, though, he sounded a bit suspicious of the girl back home. "Don't Sit Under The Apple Tree (with anyone else but me)" was a popular song in that vein. So was "Stick To Your Knittin' Kitten" — a theme that would surely strike a sour note among today's more strident advocates of women's rights and the ERA.

On the other hand, it seems to me there were many more songs in which the girl back home vowed her eternal love and fidelity. "Always In My Heart" was typical as were "I'll Be A Good Soldier Too" and "I'll Keep The Love Light Burning." I remember falling madly in love with Alice Faye when she sang "You'll Never Know (just how much I love you)" in a movie called, I believe, "The Gang's All Here." Some songs seemed to have the girl he left behind complaining a little — "Don't Get Around Much Anymore" and "Saturday Night Is the Loneliest Night Of The Week" are two of them. Some songs seemed to get a little carried away with that theme — "I Don't Want to Walk Without You" and "I'll Never Smile Again" sound a little extreme 40 years later. Then there was the one in which the girl back home gives some perfectly logical reasons why she'll be true. Referring to the men still at home she explains "They're Either Too Young Or Too Old"!

And then of course there were the "dream" songs — "I Dream Of You," "I Had The Craziest Dream," "I'll Buy That Dream," "My Dreams Are Getting Better All The Time," and just plain "Dream" which suggested dreaming as an antidote for loneliness and the blues. The moon, spoon, tune, June, croon style was passe. And, there were songs about the workers in the defense plants, too. "Rosie The Riveter," "On The Swing Shift," and "Milkman Keep Those Bottles Quiet" (about a swing shift worker complaining of lack of sleep) are some I remember.

There were hundreds more war-related songs and, of course, hundreds of songs with no war theme connection at all. There was certainly some great music in those years! Remember "In The Mood," "Blues In The Night," Tommy Dorsey's "Boogie Woogie" "Sunny Side Of The Street," "Take The 'A' Train," "Sunrise Serenade," and Clyde McCoy's "Sugar Blues"? All continue to remind me of those years and of the old home town.

Then, too, we had our share of nonsense songs that return to haunt us even after 40 years. It seems that just as you are lecturing the kids or grandkids on the difference between "real music" and that "horrible rock 'n roll racket," some disc jockey who is old enough to know better plays a "golden oldie" like "The Hut-Sut Song" or "Mairzy Doats"! There is one DJ in our area who absolutely delights in digging up that pre-war novelty song "Three Little Fishies" — complete with the baby talk, "boop boop ditum datums" and everything. It sort of destroys the point you were making about "when I was your age we had the Big Bands and beautiful music!"

I think that, of all the "war" songs, it is the hopeful, optimistic, homecoming songs that strike the most responsive chord in my memory. Songs like "It's Been A Long, Long Time" and "I'll Be Seeing You" come to mind and especially, "Sentimental Journey." My ship was in Manila Bay at the time the war ended. The city of Manila, once known as the "Pearl of the Orient," was in shambles – hardly a building was untouched and many were totally destroyed. Yet, from out of the rubble emerged musicians with assorted instruments to provide dance music for the tens of thousands of American servicemen in the area. For several weeks in the summer of '45, "Sentimental Journey" was the big hit in Manila. Then, with the Japanese surrender in Tokyo Bay, we finally knew that we would really be making that most sentimental of journeys – back home. Doris Day's beautiful, lilting arrangement with Les Brown's band never fails to fill my memory with the special, once-in-a-lifetime emotions we felt on that fantastic September day in 1945.

On my birthday in November 1945 I met Rex Pratt, from Athol, on Manila's crowded Rizal Avenue. He was in the Army and stationed just outside Manila. It was great to be able to celebrate with an old friend from home. It must have been a duzie of a day. I wish I could remember it.

A Guy Called 'Mux'

It was in Shanghai in January of '46 that I ran into Mike O'Reilly. Mike was from around Dorchester but his family used to spend their summers at Lake Mattawa before the war. His full name was Michael Ullyses Xavier O'Reilly and, in the Navy, he acquired the nickname of "Mux." I had met him once or twice in Orange before the war but he was a few years older than me so we didn't have too much in common. Our chance meeting at the Palace Hotel in Shanghai was a happy one for both of us though. We reminisced about the Athol-Orange area and later pulled liberty together on a couple of occasions.

Mux usually carried with him a little flask of a liquid he called his "secret potion." When he saw an appropriate situation he would take a swig from his flask, then hold his oversized cigarette lighter at arm's length and blow out his secret potion in an atomized mist which would ignite in a big ball of flame. It was spectacular! He said that when he was stationed in Florida he had dated the daughter of a carnival "fire eater" who taught him the trick and gave him the secret ingredients of the potion.

It was exciting pulling liberty with Mux. He wandered the streets of Shanghai belching fire like some miniature mischievous dragon in 13-button trousers. He was a cocky little Irishman who seemed to be a lightning rod for trouble. Whenever he got in a jam, however, he had only to puff his cheeks (whether or not he actually had his secret potion in his mouth) and point his cigarette lighter menacingly, and everybody backed off.

One night Mux was riding in a pedicab (the kind where the passengers sit in a seat on the front between the two wheels and the driver pedals from behind) when they got caught in a traffic jam at a major intersection. There were pedestrians, pedicabs, and rickshaws snarled up for blocks. Mux was worried about missing the last boat back to his ship and, when the Punjabi traffic cop didn't seem to be getting anywhere, Mux took matters into his own hands. Out came the flask and the lighter – and he blasted out a big ball of fire. The first blast got everyone's attention, the second opened room to move ("like parting the Red Sea," Mux recounted afterwards) and, by the third fireball, he and his driver had Nanking Road (a major thoroughfare) virtually to themselves. They careened the length of Nanking Road and, still belching fire balls, arrived at the customs jetty just as Mux used the last of his potion.

Throwing some money at his now red-eyed, smoke-singed driver, Mux raced for the liberty landing where his boat was just pulling away. He made a headlong dive to get aboard and broke off two of his front teeth on impact. When he got aboard his ship (as Mux told the story later) they woke up the ship's dentist for emergency repairs on his teeth. A Shore Patrolman and the duty Master-at-Arms helped Mux into the dentist's chair. Mux had inadvertantly swallowed some of his potion during his pedicab ride and he had a slight case of indigestion. When the dentist arrived, Mux opened his mouth and burped indelicately just as the dentist bent to examine the damage. The dentist reeled back dizzily.

"What in hell has this guy been drinking?!" he blurted.

The SP and the MAA didn't know.

"Well, I'm not putting a drill in that mouth," the dentist said emphatically. "One spark and we'll all be blown to hell!"

According to Mux, they finally opened all the portholes, turned on the fans, and had the MAA standing by with a fire extinguisher while the dentist made temporary repairs.

I ran into Mux a few weeks later. He was proud of his new teeth and said they worked better than his original ones for atomizing his secret potion. His ship left for Tsingtao a couple days later and I never saw Mux again. Several times in the summer of 1946, I looked for Mux around Lake Mattawa. I stopped and inquired about him or his family but no one had seen them. I checked a couple of times in 1947, too, but I guess he never came back. I've often thought of what a dramatic entrance we could have made at any bar or restaurant in town! And wouldn't ol' Mux have livened up Fourth of July night in Athol?! I envisioned, too, a great two-man dragon suit for Halloween with Mux belching fire and me wagging the tail. Oh well, such are the missed opportunities of life.

Chapter 6

The Summer of '46

I think there is no greater feeling of exhilaration than the anticipation of going home after a long absence. Surely one of the most fabulous days in the lives of those of my generation was the return home from World War II. For me, my homeward journey began in Shanghai, China, on April 7, 1946. The days and weeks at sea seemed like months and years before we finally reached New York near the end of May. I left my ship that very day and was processed through the Brooklyn Navy Yard for a day and half. While in Brooklyn, and still half asleep one morning, I became aware of the face being shaved in the mirror next to mine. There was something vaguely familiar about the features not covered by shaving cream. Watching the rest of the face gradually emerge I suddenly realized — "Hey! It's a guy from Athol!" About the same time Don Cookman's bleary eyes focused on my mirror and we turned to each other in surprise. We didn't have a lot of time to talk and we went our separate ways. The next time we met we were both civilians.

I was finally mustered out at the Fargo Building in Boston on Saturday June 2 and they took us over to North Station to catch the train home, our newly sewn-on "ruptured ducks" attesting to the fact that we were OUT! I met another Atholian, Eddie McGrath, at North Station and we rode home together.

Maybe it was my anxiety and impatience, but that damned B & M railroad seemed to be especially slow that day. As we rounded the last turn and Athol came into view I tried to watch from both sides of the train at once. "Hey, there's Old Main Street, and there's Athol Manufacturing, and there's the UTD — there's the shipping room where I used to work — and there's Tyler's up there, and there's Starrett's and the Town Hall, and the YMCA..." Finally the train stopped and there I was back at the familiar old depot I had left from two years before. The intervening years seemed like a bad dream, but now I was suddenly awake. This was real. This was home!

Eddie McGrath's parents drove me to Orange where my family had moved during my absence. Those first several moments with your family, as any veteran will tell you, are indescribable. Kid brothers Norm and Mac, now in high school, had grown beyond imagination in just two years as had little sister Diane. For me there was also the wonderfully strange sensation of meeting my one-and-one-half year old brother Bob for the first time — he was born while I was in the Pacific. And what a feast my mother had prepared! It was during this first 'civilized'' meal that I realized I would have to be very careful to delete my service-acquired expletives from my conversation.

I have a faded snapshot among my souvenirs of Woody Anderson, Herm Lawson and me taken a day or so after I returned. It recreates for me a little of the gratifying sensation of being home, the wonderful experience of getting ''dressed-up'' in civies again, and the joy of being out of the military service. The title ''veteran'' had a nice ring to it!

The Depot

Remembering that old railroad depot in Athol, I'm glad to hear that someone is planning to renovate and preserve it. What a wonderful idea! I hope the job is done right – with a sense of historical perspective. Oftentimes when they say they are going to preserve something here in California (an old railroad depot, for example), they tear it to the ground, build a fast food business on the site and call it ''Old Railroad Depot Hamburgers.'' The choice of name seems to satisfy their sense of responsibility to our heritage. I hope that the people of Athol will both monitor and support the depot renovation project.

For a hundred years or more, that old railroad depot must have been the hub of activity for Athol in communicating with the rest of the country. Our mail and goods arrived and left through the depot, of course, but the movement of people must have been the most important service of all.

The stories of all the countless travellers through that station would, I imagine, run the gamut of every human emotion – the apprehension and uncertainly of new immigrants arriving to start a new life and, years later, the cocky self-assurance of their children going off to college to fulfill the promise of the American dream; the tearful, reluctant, painful farewells of area youths departing for military service in several wars and the hysterical, joyous moments of homecoming when peace returned; the bright anticipation of newlyweds waving to the wedding party on the platform as they prepared to shuffle off on a honeymoon to Buffalo and Niagara Falls; and, occasionally, the pain and sadness of a casket carried from the baggage car to a waiting hearse – a casualty of war perhaps, or the final return of a wandering son.

It was always a temptation to stroll over by the depot when a train

Author in Boston, homeward bound, 1946

was due just to watch the passengers board and detrain. I think, though, that we watched with envy and planned in our most private thoughts a getaway to some fabulous vacation spot, or a rendezvous with destiny at some distant place wherever the tracks might lead, and of course a triumphal return to the old depot with fame and riches.

I remember the train engineers as being friendly, outgoing people — at least as far as kids were concerned. If you waved to one as his train was passing, more often than not he'd give you a quick "toot-toot" with his whistle. But I never lived close to the railroad tracks and the sounds that train buffs rhapsodize over are pretty much unknown to me.

About the only train whistle I was ever familiar with was the locomotive horn on Charlie Robinson's beautiful old 1936 Buick. I used to ride to and from work at the UTD with Charlie and I can remember on blizzardy mornings waiting inside my door for him to arrive. Sometimes it was storming so you could barely make out the car lights that passed along the road. Then, out of the snow and sleet would come the mournful wail of Charlie's locomotive whistle and I would run the entire length of our driveway to meet him.

The sound of a distant locomotive whistle inspires deep emotions in many people — a longing for adventure, a haunting call to be a hobo, to ride the rails on a midnight freight to Alabam', Casey Jones, 01' 97, and the Chattanooga Choo-Choo bound for glory on track 29. Not for me! Each time I hear a train whistle I think of Charlie Robinson and that old black Buick boiling out of a raging nor'easter, in the pre-dawn darkness of a New England winter, hellbent for Athol on Route 32.

Carefree Days

Looking back over the years, I think that the summer of '46 was, in many ways, one of the most carefree and delightful periods of my life. I imagine that quite a few returning veterans have the same opinion. The nation was at peace again — a peace that had come sooner than predicted. For years, military men in the Pacific had chanted "Golden Gate in '48, bread line in '49." The expectation was that we wouldn't see the Golden Gate of San Francisco until 1948, and that hard times, economically speaking, would follow within a year.

Then the atomic bomb shortened the war. The anticipated depression and its bread lines had not yet arrived in that beautiful New England summer of '46. The factories in the area were still humming away, consumer goods (except new cars) were becoming plentiful again, and rationing was a thing of the past. Though absurdly low by today's standards, most of us were earning more money than ever before in our lives. Wages had gone up in our absence and I remember my pay at the UTD was a whopping 65 cents an hour when I returned from the Navy.

Added to the feeling of relief at being safely home was a wonderful euphoria that seemed to sweep the country. It was great to be young, single, confident, and full of optimism.

I suppose every returning veteran wanted to buy a car. New cars were very slow in arriving in showrooms, however, so there was a shortage of good used cars as well. I paid quite a lot of money for a little '37 Chevy, and I remember Albine Piragis bought a powerful old Packard about the size and styling of a B & M freight car. At least there was no shortage of gas so anything that would run was put back on the road by some enterprising veteran.

Recalling that summer, I wonder if I ever spent an evening or weekend with my folks. I doubt it. There was a two-year period of wartime deprivation to make up for. We veterans were all but wallowing in money it seemed. Most of us had saved during the war — war bonds and things. Then there was the mustering out pay, and the state bonus, and terminal leave pay.

I recall those few months as a blurred and unending series of dates,

UTD shipping packers (author in center) and Mrs. Newell, about 1946

parties, and sporting events. As a virtual teetotaler for nearly 33 years now, I remember some of those times with more than just a tinge of embarrassment.

Escapades

There were some crazy things that went on in those days. Most were attributed, I think, to veterans being unable to accept the contrast between the peacefulness of the old home town and the hectic, frantic, dangerous pace of wartime.

I remember an incident in that summer of '46 involving a family dispute in the bar at the Leonard Hotel. As I recall the story, a somewhat snockered veteran was convinced that he was back in 1943 in Bizerte, North Africa. He was making a play for some woman he identified as "Dirty Gertie" when his wife walked in. An argument ensued which moved from the bar to the sidewalk, and finally across the street to the depot area.

He was trying, without much luck, to get his wife to go home when he had a flash of inspiration. With the distorted logic of his stupor he reasoned that if she had no clothes she would go home willingly to get some. With that he began stripping the clothes from his wife while a crowd quickly gathered, dissuaded from intervention by the fact that it was a family affair. I have heard many variations of the poor woman's final state of undress. By the time the police arrived to restore her modesty, she was reduced (as near as I can tell) to one shoe, one stocking, and a hair ribbon.

About a week or so after I returned home, George Kenney and I, with his dad and a couple others, went to Mechanic's Hall in Worcester to see Sugar Ray Robinson fight. That was only the first of many boxing matches that George and I attended all over New England that summer and I remember one day George, Woody Anderson, and I took my two younger brothers to Braves Field for a St. Louis Cards game.

Until TV came along, only a very small percentage of American sports fans ever actually got to see the great professional sports teams and stars. Most of the people who did lived in or near the city where the events took place. It was a rare treat and special occasion for someone from the Athol area to attend big-time sports events. Those who did would bend our ears for weeks with every little detail. There were brief sports clips at the movies, of course, but to be able to say

"It was great to be young...and full of optimism"
Don Hager, left, and Don Cookman, summer of 1946

you had seen a major league game or a title fight or championship golf or tennis made you a little special.

There were other memorable occasions and events that summer — car races in West Springfield and Keene, swimming parties at Lake Mattawa and Beaman's Pond, stage plays at the summer theater in Whalom Park, local band concerts, and concerts by the "Big Bands" like Tommy Dorsey and Vaughn Monroe in Worcester and Holyoke.

And then, too, I had some inventive friends who could dream up the wackiest things to do. There was little chance of being bored with a guy as imaginative as Don Cookman around. We were all fairly inventive but "Cookie" was the most imaginative of all. We weren't able to carry out most of his wild schemes but it was inspirational to hear his carefully plotted intrigues. There was the one where he planned to modify my car to operate with a makeshift periscope and using somebody's dog behind the wheel as the only apparent driver.

Another of his plans that comes to mind was his idea involving a large balloon and a rented dress store female manikin clad only in undergarments. The Rod and Gun Club, which, as I recall was located way out Pinedale Avenue somewhere, held a big special outdoor cookout of some sort (a clambake maybe) each summer. It was well known that a considerable quantity of beer was consumed at that function. Don's idea was to tie the scantily clad manikin to the balloon and release it, upwind of the picnic, to float over the crowd after the party had been going on a while.

The purpose was to see how many of the beer-laden gallants would take off in cars and trucks to follow the "maiden in distress" as she drifted off over the treetops on the prevailing wind. I'll bet that would have made for one exciting road race!

There was one particular idea of Don's that caught my fancy and it's too bad it never came off.

The place selected for this escapade was Winchester, N.H. I don't know why Don had it in for that little town but it was often targeted for his wildest schemes. He envisioned three or four of us arriving one day in Winchester in a station wagon bearing a sign on the sides identifying us as from an architectural company. We would have a rented surveyor's theodolite and other paraphernalia and, once in the center of town, we would set up as though to survey. We planned that, whenever any of the locals came close to see what was going on, one of us would say to another in an authoritative voice such things as:

"We're going to have to tear down that church!" or

"That town hall is going to have to go!" or

"We'll move that big yellow house to the left about 100 feet."

Whenever anyone asked, we would tell them that a new big highway was to be constructed through the town. When we were sure that we had stirred up a hornet's nest of rumor, we would pack up our equipment and drive away leaving little old Winchester puzzled and concerned, maybe even panicky, about its future. It was fun to imagine how many baffled state and congressional figures would have been harangued and threatened by the people of Winchester.

All of Don's schemes were planned down to the smallest detail but he could improvise quickly when a new situation arose. He and I planned, one hot summer day, to stir up some mischief at the UTD shipping room where we were both employed. Our boss, Matt Meany was away on vacation. During the noon hour Don went home and put on his swimming trunks under his shorts. The plan was for him to take off his trousers in the men's room (located next to the time clock), hand them to me, and then to chase me out into the shipping room demanding his pants back just as all the ladies from the office were lined up to punch out.

About 2 o'clock, though, Mr. Meany's secretary remarked how terribly hot it was. Quick to seize a golden opportunity, Don agreed that it was hot — so hot, he said he thought he'd take his pants off. And he did. Then carefully creasing them and folding them over his arm he strolled the whole length of the office. We heard the screams and shrieks of the ladies all the way down in the packing section. I'm not sure if any ladies really fainted but it certainly caused a commotion. Mr. Meany returned from vacation the next Monday and Don left the UTD that very week. I'm not sure if the two incidents were related.

When autumn came that year, I decided it was time for a change of scenery. That October, Woody Anderson and I went off to Florida — to seek our fortune, I guess. Woody found the lovely girl who was to become his wife and I found myself broke within a few months and came home for Christmas and stayed.

In 1947, things were not quite as good for me in Athol as they had been in the summer of '46. There were no more government bonuses, all the war bonds had been chased and spent, and the "big" 65-cents-an-hour wages were gone. Old friends were getting married and starting families, others were going off to college, and some simply moved away to find better jobs. I guess the most noteworthy thing I did that year was learn to fly.

By the winter of 1947-48, I and a lot of other veterans were working at jobs like cutting ice on the lakes for the two ice companies in town and unloading freight cars for Tyler's. Many of us joined the "52-20 Club" – a federal umemployment compensation plan that paid $20 a week for 52 weeks.

There were some good times, too. I think we discovered that it doesn't necessarily take a whole lot of money to have a good time – only good friends. I have fond memories of a few winter evenings spent in the lounge of the Pequoig Hotel harmonizing on old songs for hours with friends like Don Hager, Pete Tandy, Sonny Hames, Al Cullen, Clinton Fitch and others. Clint, as I recall, was an exasperation to us. A delightful guy who knew all the words to every song, it seemed he could never find the right key. Our accusations of tone deafness did not dampen his enthusiasm one iota. His lusty off-key rendition of "When You Wore a Tulip" rings in my ear to this day.

The good times became fewer, however, and my future less promising in the Athol area. In March 1948, I re-enlisted in the Navy. A few months later my family moved west to Washington State and my close family ties with Athol were permanently severed. Except for a few very brief visits of a few hours' duration, I did not return to the Athol area for more than 36 years.

Chapter 7

There's No Place Like Home

My desire to return to the scenes of my youth had grown increasingly acute as I committed my recollections to paper. By the time I sent them to Athol Daily News Editor Barney Cummings, I knew I would have to make the trip – despite Thomas Wolfe's oft-quoted admonition that "you can't go home again." On May 22, 1984, I went back to New England for my first real visit in 36 years.

I rented a car at Bradley International Airport (in Windsor Locks, Conn.) and drove to Petersham. It was a rainy night with patches of fog and the Daniel Shays Highway (which for some reason I remembered as being a four-lane road) was virtually deserted. As I neared the forested outskirts of Petersham on Route 122, I began looking for West Street. Finally, through the mist and rain, I spotted a road on the left and made the turn, still unsure of where I was after so many years. I drove rather gingerly along in the rain and fog and suddenly I came to a "Y" in the road. I knew then that I wasn't on West Street. But where was I? I stopped the car in a moment of rising uncertainty and peered through the rainy night trying to get my bearings. And then, off to my right, the fog drifted aside to reveal, like a ghostly apparition, the lovely old Petersham Center School. There it was, wreathed in fog patches, framed in all its elegance against the black sky – and the unexpected sight just took the breath right out of me. I could not even purposely have chosen a more appropriate or heart-tugging reference point.

I don't know how long I sat there taking in the handsome lines of

Petersham's Center School (drawing by Barbara Ellis)

that beautiful building. The old well house, the curved driveway, the projecting roof under which the school buses let us out in inclement weather, the dormer windows of the alcoves on the second floor, and the little gymnasium — all fitted in precisely with the mental image I had carried for more than 40 years.

The drifting mist momentarily obscured the school from view and blew quickly away again to reveal in my mind's eye an autumn scene from a long remembered year. Miss Amsden's free-hand drawing class was sitting on the grass and on the stone wall sketching trees, the well house or each other. The faces of my sophomore classmates in all their beaming teenage tenderness came quickly and easily to mind. A wisp of fog, a fading vision and then in the mirror of my mind another scene from the autumn of 1941 — recess and most of the high school boys playing football on the school's front lawn (being very wary of the huge protruding rock at about the imaginary 40-yard line). The game, as usual, pitted the Class of '42 against the rest of the school. We (the rest of the school) had very little chance against athletes like Herm Lawson, Ben LePoer, Joe Avery, Pete Barnes, Horace Coolidge and the other seniors.

The approach of a car along Spring Street snapped me out of my reverie and I continued on, knowing now exactly where I was. By now it was 11:30 p.m. and the streets were deserted. I stopped briefly in the center of town in front of the old town hall. I knew that it was really a recently constructed exact replica of the historic one I had known. A terrible fire in the '60s had destroyed the original. If I had not read of the disaster, though, I would never have realized I was now looking at a copy.

Miss Flint's Crosley

I had reserved a room in "Winterwood at Petersham" — the charming inn newly opened by Robert and Jean Day on North Main Street. I realized, as I arrived, that Winterwood had once been the home of Susan Flint, a spinster, who was considered a sort of eccentric during my years in Petersham. My recollection of her is one of active and dedicated civic interest and service. My contemporaries' recollections of Susan Flint, however, center on the little Crosley automobile that she drove in the '40s. I guess it must have been the first of what we now call "subcompact" cars. A favorite prank among town teenagers was for a half dozen strong young men to wait until she was in a store shopping and pick up up her little car and put it on the sidewalk.

One day a group of Petersham teenagers driving around Athol spotted Susan's car parked on Exchange Street. Quickly stopping their own car, they hastily converged on the little Crosley and, after checking in both directions for signs of Susan or the police, they hurriedly bounced her car up onto the sidewalk. Then, just as they were brushing their hands and congratulating one another on their strength and cleverness, one of them noticed that the car was occupied! Gathering around the car they peered incredulously at a little old lady sitting in the passenger's seat. She must have been a very elderly friend or relative who was waiting for Susan to return. With wide wondering eyes and wobbly head she stared from window to window at her assaulters who stared back with alarm and embarrassment.

Unable to find appropriate words, and feeling that an apology was quite useless in any case, the now chastened mischief makers quickly and wordlessly lifted the little car as gently as possible and placed it once again at the curb. They then backed away to their own car, waving politely and grinning sickly apologies to their poor baffled victim. That may have been the last time anyone manhandled Susan Flint's Crosley. I wonder if that poor little old lady ever tried to tell anyone what had happened. She'd have had a tough time convincing most people and would probably have been accused of advancing senility.

On my first morning back in the old home town, I arose early, had a lovely breakfast at Winterwood, and then took a stroll around the village. It was a beautiful day — the rain had gone, the sun was bright, the sky blue, and the trees in full, lush foliage. It was New England in the fullness of its springtime splendor.

Petersham Common

How fulfilling it is to return to familiar scenes — especially when those scenes hold so many warm memories! The center of Petersham is exactly as I remember it from the 1940s. The old Nichewaug Inn (now the Maria Assumpta Academy) is as handsome as ever. The bandstand still dominates the center of the common. My! What memories that little building revives of warm summer nights, the common ringed with family cars, children romping on the green, teenagers strolling arm-in-arm, Hutchinson's Country Store doing a land office business in soda pop, candy bars, and popcorn, and Basil Coolidge directing the band and doing the vocal honors. For me, a concert by the Rolling Stones or the Boston Pops couldn't hold a candle to the 1940s Petersham Brass Band.

On this bright morning, I noticed small flags flying beside rocks placed at the foot of many of the trees in the common. Upon inspection I found that the rocks bore brass markers, each commemorating a Petersham casualty of war. I knelt and read every one of them and, at some, images of young faces crossed my mind. They were the faces of friends who so many years ago left this quiet lovely, peaceful town and gave up their lives in far-off places like Iwo Jima and Luxembourg.

My emotions were mixed as I read the names and dates and places of death. There was a sense of pride at having known some of these men. I remembered them with a certain reverence and affection and a sense of sorrow that they had been cut down as life was only beginning. But then came a sudden, jarring emotion — "better them than me" — and I felt a quick pang of guilt for having let such a thought enter my head. Upon reflection, however, I knew that, given the choice, each would have preferred to live their full lives and, in middle age, themselves kneel at a marker to MY memory. They had not chosen to die. It was their fate, their destiny, and His will. It was mine to live, to have a family, to grow old, to carry with me a warm and loving memory of the place where we had shared a few years of youth — and to return one day to pause and reflect and remember.

The Unitarian Church stood against the azure morning sky like a classic picture postcard. As I walked past and started down West Street I noticed something strange about the church horse shed. As a matter of fact, it's no longer a horse shed. I peeked in and discovered that it is now a large dining/meeting room.

A Halloween Trick

I wonder what they ever did with that old horse-drawn fire buggy that was stored there during all the years I lived in Petersham. That fire buggy got only one workout a year that I can recall. That was on Halloween night. It was a ritual that the old vehicle be stolen as the highlight of the evening. For the life of me, I cannot remember ever going trick-or-treating — it was trick or nothing in those days and nobody was given a choice.

"Pick" Preble was the police chief and, as I recall, he was also the fire chief, truant officer, dog officer, and probably held several other offices. On Halloween night, Pick maintained a steady patrol of all the streets in his pick-up truck (Petersham could not afford, or had little need of, a cruiser in those days).

At some time in the evening, when we thought Pick had been lured away to another part of town, we would make a mad dash for the church horse shed. A gang of boys would disappear noisily into the shed all the while "shushing" one another and stumbling into things in the dark. In a moment or two they would come out dragging the old fire buggy.

The ride down West Street hill might have been calamitous. There was always someone, however, who knew how to operate the brake and prevent running over the guys who were trotting along in front doing the steering. There was not enough room to accommodate everyone who wanted to ride, but it was fun just to run alongside and be a part of the action.

At the bottom of the hill everyone had to dismount and lend a hand pushing or pulling up the next hill. Usually we got only as far as Lewis Street when Pick Preble would arrive back on the scene. We would see from a distance his spotlight casting about the sidewalks. He would speed up and come racing to the spot when he finally saw where we were. As he approached, we'd leave the wagon and scatter in all directions amid shrieks and yells and screams. Then Pick would stop by the wagon, hook it to his pick-up truck, and tow it back to the church horse shed for another year.

Before departing, the policeman would peer menacingly at stone walls, and bushes or other places where he knew we were hiding. Sometimes he would play his spotlight over likely hiding places and we would hold our breaths in apprehension of capture. Actually, in remembering those Halloween nights, I think old Pick Preble had it all planned and orchestrated. I think he knew exactly when to be "lured" away and when to return to retrieve the wagon. I'm sure he had no intention of disciplining us — his threatening search was meant only to add excitement and a sense of adventure to our Halloween.

I must have walked for an hour or more on that lovely spring morning. Each turning provided fresh memories; each step seemed to carry me back further in time. I returned to Winterwood, got the car, and spent another hour or two driving up and down every street and road in town. By the end of the morning I was feeling almost like a kid again.

I decided that the lunch hour would be the most convenient time to drop in on John LePoer at the Center School. A few days before leaving California I had received a long letter from John. It seemed better to answer it with a visit in person. I walked up the steps and through the two sets of doors of the handsome old school and suddenly it seemed like old home week. There was, besides John, old school chums Doris (Nelson) Coolidge, Annie (Mitchell) LePoer, and Maggie (Waid) Lundquist. Annie called up husband Ben and he came over to the school. What a treasured moment!

I think the strangest aspect of that visit was walking into the principal's office for other than disciplinary reasons. Everything in the office seemed little changed in the intervening 40-odd years. The main difference was that instead of cowering before the baleful glare of the volatile "Pop" Arnold, I was engaged in happy conversation with my benign and amiable friend, John LePoer.

It was in that very office that Mr. Arnold had told me one day "turn in your books, get out of school, and don't come back!" Thinking I was about to be exposed, I had impulsively confessed to smoking on the school grounds (with visiting friends from Athol – Albine Piragis and Rex Pratt). I went home and my dad suggested that if I went back the next day and apologized, Mr. Arnold might let me return. I did and he did. My books were still where I had left them on his desk.

John invited me to stay for lunch in the cafeteria downstairs. I never got lunch there when I was a student. In fact, there was no cafeteria then – only a home economics room. I was reminded of another confrontation with Mr. Arnold that occurred right outside the door to that room. It was the night of a basketball game and someone from the team got into a case of state-furnished canned grapefruit. The first I knew of that, however, was when Herm Lawson said "Here, Ken, have some grapefruit," and thrust a half-empty can in my hand. I should have suspected something was amiss. Herm had many admirable traits and attributes, but I don't recall generosity being near the top of the list. Hardly had I started to eat the first spoonful when Mr. Arnold appeared like a magical menacing genie glaring intently at my spoon. "Take off your uniform," he growled as he grabbed the can away. "You're no longer on this team!"

I had my uniform half off when he sent word that I was still part of the team and could keep my uniform on. The other members of the team had gone to him and confessed their participation. He couldn't fire the whole team – he had a basketball game to play.

Mine was not an illustrious athletic record at Petersham High. Basketball was the only team sport in which I participated – my height being my primary recommendation for a place on the team. I was, you might say, a "crisis" player. Coach Nickerson saved me just for those urgent crisis situations – like when Petersham got too far ahead.

In going through my old "Hilltop" yearbooks, I found that I never scored a point – nor even tried to as near as I can tell. Coach Nickerson made me a "stationary guard." He showed me which end of the court was the other team's and told me to stand around under that basket and stay out of the way of teammates Ben and Herm and Joe and Pete. I never earned a letter in basketball. My only reward, when I left the game, was hearing our little cheerleaders yell "Yea Ken! Yea Richards! Yea, Yea, Ken Richards!" I was never sure if they were cheering my performance or the fact that I was being taken out of the game.

Petersham High had a pretty good team for a little school. I remember one night we beat Hardwick 15 to 2 on their court! Can you imagine that? A team scoring only 2 points in a BASKETBALL game! My kids' Little League BASEBALL games often had scores far bigger than 15 to 2! It's too bad Hardwick scored at all. A shutout in basketball would surely have made sports history.

As I drove out of the school yard after my lunch with John, a long forgotten wish came back to me. I remembered how badly I had wanted a car of my own during my high school days. Only two or three Petersham students had cars, however, and I presume the same was true in all but the most affluent communities in that day and age. I realize now that it probably was good for us to have to walk. It wasn't a case of laziness that created the urge to ride – it was the status. Of course the automobile is as much a status symbol today as it was then, but in those days we'd settle for almost anything that ran. And, in most cases, you had to earn it yourself. I never knew anyone whose parents bought them a car.

On the way over to Athol I recalled how many times I had jogged over that route from the time I entered high school until I joined the

Navy. During that period I had lived just around the corner from the Harvard Forestry School which I guess is about halfway between Athol and Petersham. My pal Woody Anderson lived at the Harvard School. Many's the night we ran home from the gym in Petersham after basketball practice. And even more times we ran home from Athol after a movie at the York. In those days we jogged to get from point A to point B — not just because it was a fad. And we didn't need any fancy shoes, jogging suits, or headbands, either. We didn't even need to get "psyched" up for it. Drifting snow, gale-force winds, and a wind chill factor of 65 degrees below zero does wonders for your motivation around midnight!

As I passed the Harvard Forest I recalled the many happy hours I spent there with Woody and his family. There was a ping pong table in the basement and Woody, Cliff Upham, Dave Thomas and I learned to play the game there. I remember one night Cliff and I were playing and he stopped suddenly saying he smelled smoke. I sniffed the air and agreed, so we put down our paddles to look around. We found the fire all right — it was in the pocket of my trousers! That was the last time I ever carried hard wintergreen mints and kitchen matches in the same pocket!

Reminiscing In Athol

My first stop in Athol was the police station to look up my old buddy Don Hager. His surprise at seeing me was complete. He said he hoped I wasn't going to ask him to go flying. He introduced me around to Chief Jillson and others and to Dan Watson, the veterans affairs officer, down the hall. It was Dan who confirmed for me that Bobby Adams had died in the explosion of the ammunition ship USS Mount Hood in November 1944.

Don and I were so busy reminiscing about old times that I never did make it upstairs in the Memorial Building. I had wanted to visit the rotunda again to see if it was as impressive as I remembered.

Don took the rest of the afternoon off and we drove over just about every street in town in the next two or three hours. We made one stop at the "old town hall" which now houses the Athol Historical Society. There we met Dexter Gleason who, with real pride in the exhibits, gave us a brief tour of the place. Oh, how I'd love to spend a few days there looking in every nook and cranny! I wonder how many Atholians have taken the time to visit that historic building and its artifacts. That will be a scheduled "must" stop for me on my next trip home. I intend to take Dexter up on his invitation for a guided tour.

As we drove around town, Don was able to fill me in on what used to be where. We stopped once along Old Main Street to look down at the UTD, where I used to work. I had a strange feeling that I had never seen that particular view before. And then I realized that I was looking right through where Tyler's sash and blind factory was supposed to be! It was gone! Don assured me that Tyler's really had been there once and that I was not imagining things.

Driving down Grove Street I pointed out the shortcut we used to take to the Highland School. Just above where the railing ends you could slip through, go carefully down the bank to the bottom of the gully, and follow a path to Auburn Place and the school yard. In the winter it was great fun sliding down but difficult climbing back up on your way home. In the spring, when the sides of the gully turned soft, it was dangerous. If you slipped and tumbled to the muck and mire at the bottom, you staggered to school caked with mud, dripping wet, and looking somewhat like a miniature "Creature from the Black Lagoon." After the second or third occurrence, Miss Bonnett's sympathy began to wear a little thin and she made you stay after school to make up for the time you spent drying off.

Now the school is gone and I could find no trace of the old "gully path" that uptown kids had followed for generations. I'll bet the shortcut from uptown to the Riverbend School down over the ledges from Bliss Street is still in use, though. Kids will always find the shortest way.

That afternoon, Don and I also followed the route that used to be "posted" for sliding in the winter from Highland Street to Glen Street to Kennebunk Street to Green Street. That made for a great ride on your "Flexible Flyer" or "Flying Arrow" sled. I wonder if the argument still rages over which are the faster – round or flat runners. Of course, the fastest vehicle was a full-sized travois loaded with adults. A half-ton of humanity and hardwood on steel runners can develop a tremendous rate of speed on a hill like Highland Street. I recall, though, that the acute angle from Glen Street to continue down to Green Street was too great for some sleds, and most travoises turned left (uphill) on Kennebunk Street.

I remember one night a travois tried to negotiate a right turn, failed, hurtled over the snow-covered stone wall, and wound up spilling people all over Police Chief Callahan's backyard. The travois driver had been warming himself internally with the contents of a Prohibition-era flask and went into an absolute panic as a light came on and Chief Callahan came to the door to see what was going on. The driver was convinced that the Chief would run him in for driving under the influence of alcohol. He didn't, of course, and the driver breathed a mighty sigh of relief when the Chief put out his light and went back in the house.

All in all Don and I had a great afternoon of reliving old times. After accepting Jean Hager's invitation to stay for dinner, I contacted old pal Albine Piragis and spent a most enjoyable evening with him and wife Topsy — again rehashing the wild and wooly days of our youth. I brought with me some letters he had written to my parents during his service on a cruiser in World War II.

That Friday evening I picked up my brother Norm at Bradley Airport. Norm is an executive with Marathon Oil Company and a freelance author on the side. His publisher had just announced the publication of his two latest books the day before he flew east to share my vacation in the old home town.

The Old Homestead

On Saturday Norm and I drove over to Winchendon and Waterville. The houses where we lived in 1932 and '33 are still there. Winchendon's Tucker School where I entered the first grade in 1932 is gone now, but we drove by the old Woodcock School in Waterville which our dad attended from 1911 to 1916 and which I attended in 1933. It has been restored and redesigned as an attractive apartment house.

Our main purpose that day, however, was to visit the site of the little town of New Boston which was razed many years ago to make way for the Birch Hill Dam project. In the last few months of my dad's life he and I had been working on a map and description of New Boston as he remembered it. Dad died before we could get it finished, but I had the rough sketches and notes with me on my trip home.

The Richards farm occupied much of the land all around the point where Alger Road dead-ends at New Boston Road. There is little trace of the farm today. Where dense brush and small trees now extend

The Richards homestead in New Boston (about 1930)

from the road to Priest Brook was the site of the "big barn" and open meadows and cow pastures when my dad lived there. The farm house was situated on the north side of Alger Road and the "small barn" on the south side. On the hill behind the house was an apple orchard and above that a field filled with berry bushes. Now it is woods. Some stone walls exist today to indicate where the small barn stood and some very old fruit trees still grow to the east of the barn site. I wondered if my dad had climbed in these branches as a child. Many of the stories of my grandfather's feats of strength center on this spot – usually involving the lifting of farm animals and machinery. At that corner in front of the house, my dad told me, he and my uncle and aunts would race to stand and watch the passing of the earliest automobiles. In that quiet pastoral environment, the noise of those old cars could be heard long before they arrived.

My dad had regaled me with stories and descriptions of life on the farm from the time I was old enough to understand. He had told me of the children of New Boston being picked up by a horse-drawn "barge" and carried to the Woodcock School a couple of miles away in Waterville. He told of cutting ice on Lake Dennison in the winter and of family picnics there in the summer. He described many of the local characters from that era such as the 375-pound neighbor who collapsed and died while sitting on a bedpan. And there was the turn-of-the-century "flower child" who spoke only in rhyme. He would go to Sibley's store and place an order like, "Mr. Sibley, if you please, I would like two pounds of cheese," or "From the baker, 'ere I'm dead; I would like a loaf of bread." According to my dad's recollections, the fellow even cursed in rhyme. He told me, too, of King Philip's Rock at the edge of Priest Brook, beneath which, it is said, two Colonial children hid for a couple of days from marauding Indians.

Norm and I spent an hour or more at the site of the old farm. We looked in vain for the huge flat stone that had been the doorstep of the house — put in place by my grandfather and a team of horses. But if no physical evidence of the family homestead remained, in the stillness of a warm spring afternoon it was easy to create a mental image of a long-since faded scene. That of a hard-working, honest, and moral New England farm family struggling against an unpredictable economy and extremes of nature to survive and perhaps even to prosper a little.

I saw in my mind's eye a little boy of 5 or 6 who had his mother's features, barefoot and wearing only overalls, following his ponderous and powerful father at his chores. I could visualize that little boy skipping down New Boston Road rolling a hoop, free of care and unconcerned about the future. It would have been inconceivable then for him to even imagine that one day his aging sons would stand at that quiet spot seeking, in some sensory way, to bridge the gap of time between the ages. With today's younger generation of Richardses scattered throughout the world, it may be that Norm and I are the last of Fred and Jenny's descendents who will ever visit the site of their homestead. Perhaps the last frail thread linking the present and future with that quiet, lovely spot has unravelled forever. I'm not sure how Norm felt, but I drove away with a sense of sadness.

Memorial Day in Petersham

I had looked with great anticipation to Memorial Day in Petersham. I remember it as an important day of the year that attracted large numbers of people to the ceremonies. Five minutes before the start of the parade it began to rain and Grand Marshall George "Piggy" Brunelle made the decision to move the affair inside the town hall.

I wonder how on earth George ever got the nickname "Piggy" in his school days. It suggests slovenliness and gluttony, neither of which describe the George Brunelle I have known for more than 40 years. I'll have to aske him next time I see him.

Other friends also had nicknames of obscure origin like, for example, Ben "Shaw" LePoer, Herm "Worm" Lawson, Albine "Beak" Piragis, Herbie "Sheep" Lamb, George "Bingo" Barnes, and Bernard "Bumps" Barnes to name a few. My nickname in high school was "Lunky" – a word that, I think, connoted the degree of elegance and finesse in my carriage, bearing and general demeanor at that age. It was given me in good natured jest by Carl Robinson, a droll and witty friend who died in his junior year of high school. It was an apt nickname and a few friends still remember it.

The memorial ceremony in the town hall at Petersham was a moving experience for me. Despite the rain, there was a near capacity crowd. The band played some great old traditional pieces and the clergy made some wonderfully appropriate remarks. There was a uniformed color guard and a rifle unit and uniformed members of the American Legion Women's Auxiliary. The participants ranged in age from school children to the elderly.

I suppose all of those things are common to Memorial Day celebrations in most cities and towns. But there was a wonderful feature of Petersham's service that can only happen in a small town. That is reading the name of every person from the town who served in the armed forces in time of war. It is a tradition that, I suppose, goes way back to when Memorial Day was first celebrated. It is gratifying to know that a hundred years from now my name may still be spoken once each year only in that quiet little New England village. How wonderful it would be if no names were ever added to those now repeated each Memorial Day.

I was especially impressed by the sincerity and respectful attention of those in the audience. Every man, woman, and child in that hall listened attentively to every speech, every prayer, and to every name recited from the honor roll. Ruth Bassingthwaite recited "Where Poppies Grow in Flanders Fields." I had not heard or read that moving poem in over 40 years. I can remember it being a part of every Memorial Day exercise in every school I ever attended. At one point the band played and the audience sang "America the Beautiful." By that time, however, my emotions had overtaken me. I opened my mouth to sing and not a sound came out. I haven't felt so strongly that love of country or national pride or thankfulness for what I have in many a long year. At that moment, in that hall, amid that chorus of lusty and fervent voices, everything that is good about America seemed to fill one's heart and swell one's pride with a richness beyond all material things. That moment was worth the trip from California.

Near the end of the ceremony, the rifle unit went out on the front steps of the hall and fired a salute. The audience stood as one in silent reverence as a bugler on the steps played "Taps." A moment of silence was followed by an answering bugler playing "Taps" from the Village Cemetery. The notes of that distant trumpet, muted by the dampness, came softly through the falling rain to mark the end of the service. I felt wrung out emotionally.

After the service, I had a wonderful opportunity to meet and chat with lots of old friends I had not seen in many years. It's strange that the sharpest memory most of them have of me is my inordinate fear of snakes. Each had a tale to tell of my panic in the presence of reptiles. Glenn Lawson reminded me of the day in school when someone displayed a rubber snake (I thought it was real) and (as Glenn tells it) I was out the door, around the school, and was past third base and on my way to left field before they convinced me it was fake. Cliff Upham reminded me of a party that Lewis Babbitt threw for the young folks in town. Mr. Babbitt, who collected snakes for a living, hid in a great nest of them during some sort of game like hide 'n seek. The vision of that cage opening and Mr. Babbitt standing up, alive with snakes of every description, haunts me to this day. Ann LePoer, whose parents delivered the mail to and from Athol reminded me of the day her mother, Mrs. Withington, gave me a ride home. She did not tell me until I got out of the car that I had been sitting on a box of 16 copperheads that Mr. Babbitt was mailing off.

The remaining two days of my visit were anti-climactic after the emotional impact of Memorial Day. On the day after, Don Hager rode along as I took Norm to the airport in Connecticut and Jean put on a terrific meal on our return. That evening good friends Cliff and Judy Upham, John and Ann LePoer, George and Marilee Brunelle, and Ben and Annie LePoer joined me at Winterwood for a terrific evening of remembering old times and bringing me up to date on happenings over the intervening decades since I went away.

It was still raining the next morning as I prepared to leave. Just as I was walking out the door, a call came from George Brunelle. "Hold everything," he said. He had succeeded in borrowing sister Kathryn's copy of "A History of Petersham" that I wanted so very much to read. In a few moments, he arrived to deliver that precious book.

I took one last drive through town and by the school as I headed back to California filled with warm memories and happy thoughts. I have traveled to and lived in many places on this old earth in the past 40 years – experiences that mostly I do not regret. But as I turned left onto Daniel Shays Highway and headed for Bradley Field the words of an old, old song came back to me. How true they are: "There's no place like home!"

Epilogue

The experience of returning to a truly loved and well remembered place after an absence of more than 36 years can, of course, happen only once in a lifetime. The anticipation of such an experience, happy as it may be, is mixed with doubts and misgivings. Will, for example, anyone remember you? Will you remember everyone you meet?

I found that the most difficult problem was accepting the fact that old friends and relatives have also aged. Because I had not seen many of them for three and a half decades, the only image that I had of them was terribly out of date. I tended to remember them as virile, vigorous, and virginal, with full heads of hair and smooth complexions, shapely young women and svelte young men.

Despite what common sense would dictate, I found myself unaccountably shaken to find that in most cases they had aged as much as I. Their hair, too, is thinning, greying, or mostly gone. Little "crow's feet" are framing their eyes too, and "liver spots" have also blotched their hands. They, too, move at a slower pace. Only a few remain lithe and vibrant.

Of course, their image of me dated back to 1948 or beyond. On a couple of occasions, old friends and I stared at one another for long moments, finding in each other's features a vague resemblance to someone we knew we had met before. It was usually easier for me to recognize them because I was searching. For them, not having an inkling that I was even in the country, it must have seemed a little like coming face-to-face with the Ghost of Christmas Past.

When last I left them, they were filled with the hopes and dreams of the young. Some were young marrieds already contributing to the post-war baby boom. Their eyes shone then with the promise of a happy life, a future brimming with plans and goals. Now that future is the past.

I returned thinking, I suppose, in my sub-conscious mind, to find the past. Perhaps for a moment we could turn back the sands of time. If we told enough stories, laughed hard enough, remembered more details, recalled a few more half-forgotten names, perused more yearbooks and photo albums, and shook our head more wonderingly at our remembered and exaggerated escapades, perhaps – just perhaps – the years would drop away and we'd be young again.

It doesn't work, of course, but to share those wonderful moments of recollection with good and dear friends is, I think, the next best thing to reliving your youth. If our memories differed somewhat in certain particulars, that was to be expected. Memory becomes less and less precise as the years pass and no doubt some of my recollections have slipped considerably away from events as they truly happened. And, too, we all tend to interpret events in our own individual way. Sometimes about all we can agree on years later is that an event DID happen. The why, where, when, who, and how are subject to the vagaries of human memory.

In any case, accuracy is not the most necessary ingredient in rehashing childhood events. The spontaneously triggered, random recollections of our personal lives need no precise definition. Besides, we like to spice and season our retold tales to enliven a story or to reinforce the persona of a character from our past. We tend naturally to attach greater virtues and strengths to those in our memory who we most loved or respected. And we are apt to paint the disagreeable characters from our past in darker tones and to emphasize their weaknesses and imperfections. If it helps hold a listener's ear, a little exaggeration is probably excusable.

I know that I will never return permanently to the area north of Quabbin. I have now been in California for more years than I lived in New England and I will probably live out the rest of my years on the Monterey Peninsula. But I am a New Englander, born and bred, and proud of it. The memories of my youth, the good times and the not-so-good, will always be with me.

The family fables that I have repeated from my Yankee ancestors will continue to be passed down by my California descendants. And some of MY stories of New England will be remembered and added to the family folklore. Those stories, though perhaps imprecisely recalled, are simply the special memories of one member of an all too rapidly aging generation. They are the random recollections of a boy who grew to manhood amid a large and loving family and a host of cherished friends in a distant, quieter place in a simpler, more innocent time.

About the Author

Kenneth G. Richards was born in Orange and lived in several Central Massachusetts towns during his childhood years including Waterville (a section of Winchendon), Templeton, Gardner, Petersham and Athol. He served in the U.S. Navy during World War II and returned to live in the Mt. Grace area until rejoining the Navy in 1948. He retired from active duty in 1966 to take up a career as a writer and editor.

He is the author of 15 children's books and has also written dozens of magazine articles, mostly on history or military subjects, as well as numerous multi-media social studies and science educational programs. He is a member of the Society for Technical Communications. He is Chief of Reports at the U.S. Army Combat Developments Experimentation Center at Ford Ord, California.

He is married to the former Joy Melrose of Carmel, California. They have three sons living on the West Coast and a daughter in Athens, Greece. Ken and Joy live in Pebble Beach on California's central coast.

Other Millers River Books

"Ez, Or, Lovemaking, Horsetrading and Fighting in Swift River Valley," by William H. Walker. (Yankee humor from the valley flooded to make the Quabbin Reservoir.)

"Profiles of the Past: An Illustrated History of Ashburnham, Gardner, Hubbardston, Templeton, Westminster and Winchendon, Massachusetts," by Tom Malloy, illustrated by Jim Murphy.

"North of Quabbin: A Guide to Nine Massachusetts Towns," by Allen Young. (Including Athol, Erving, New Salem, Orange, Petersham, Phillipston, Royalston, Warwick and Wendell plus Quabbin history and information.)

Coming soon: Illustrated guidebooks to the regions around Brattleboro, Vt.; Keene, N.H.; Greenfield, Mass.; Shelburne Falls, Mass.; and Northampton, Mass.

Write to Box 159, Athol MA 01331, for a free mail-order catalog.

About the Publisher

Millers River Publishing Co. was founded in 1983 by writer/editor Allen Young for the creation and publication of fine books about the New England of today and yesterday. Our name honors the Millers River, a Connecticut River tributary, a primary natural resource of the North Central Massachusetts Region we call home. We chose this name to reflect the "love of place" that has long been characteristic of New England's people.

This book was typeset in Garth Graphic Condensed. Typesetting, printing and binding were done at the facilities of the Athol Daily News and Highland Press in Athol, Massachusetts.